Coping with Faculty Stress

Peter Seldin, *Editor*
Pace University

NEW DIRECTIONS FOR TEACHING AND LEARNING
KENNETH E. EBLE, *Editor-in-Chief*
University of Utah, Salt Lake City

Number 29, Spring 1987

Paperback sourcebooks in
The Jossey-Bass Higher Education Series

Jossey-Bass Inc., Publishers
San Francisco • London

Peter Seldin (ed.).
Coping with Faculty Stress.
New Directions for Teaching and Learning, no. 29.
San Francisco: Jossey-Bass, 1987.

New Directions for Teaching and Learning
Kenneth E. Eble, *Editor-in-Chief*

New Directions for Teaching and Learning is published quarterly
by Jossey-Bass Inc., Publishers. *New Directions* is numbered
sequentially—please order extra copies by sequential number. The
volume and issue numbers above are included for the convenience
of libraries. Second-class postage paid at San Francisco, California,
and at additional mailing offices. POSTMASTER: Send address
changes to Jossey-Bass Inc., Publishers, 433 California Street,
San Francisco, California 94104.

Editorial correspondence should be sent to the Editor-in-Chief,
Kenneth E. Eble, Department of English, University of Utah,
Salt Lake City, Utah 84112.

Library of Congress Catalog Card Number LC 85-644763

International Standard Serial Number ISSN 0271-0633

International Standard Book Number ISBN 1-55542-975-0

Cover art by WILLI BAUM

Manufactured in the United States of America

Ordering Information

The paperback sourcebooks listed below are published quarterly and can be ordered either by subscription or single copy.

Subscriptions cost $40.00 per year for institutions, agencies, and libraries. Individuals can subscribe at the special rate of $30.00 per year *if payment is by personal check.* (Note that the full rate of $40.00 applies if payment is by institutional check, even if the subscription is designated for an individual.) Standing orders are accepted.

Single copies are available at $9.95 when payment accompanies order. (California, New Jersey, New York, and Washington, D.C., residents please include appropriate sales tax.) For billed orders, cost per copy is $9.95 plus postage and handling.

Substantial discounts are offered to organizations and individuals wishing to purchase bulk quantities of Jossey-Bass sourcebooks. Please inquire.

Please note that these prices are for the academic year 1986–1987 and are subject to change without notice. Also, some titles may be out of print and therefore not available for sale.

To ensure correct and prompt delivery, all orders must give either the *name of an individual* or an *official purchase order number.* Please submit your order as follows:

Subscriptions: specify series and year subscription is to begin.
Single Copies: specify sourcebook code (such as, TL1) and first two words of title.

Mail orders for United States and Possessions, Latin America, Canada, Japan, Australia, and New Zealand to:
Jossey-Bass Inc., Publishers
433 California Street
San Francisco, California 94104

Mail orders for all other parts of the world to:
Jossey-Bass Limited
28 Banner Street
London EC1Y 8QE

New Directions for Teaching and Learning Series
Kenneth E. Eble, *Editor-in-Chief*

TL1   *Improving Teaching Styles,* Kenneth E. Eble
TL2   *Learning, Cognition, and College Teaching,* Wilbert J. McKeachie
TL3   *Fostering Critical Thinking,* Robert E. Young

Contents

Editor's Notes

Outsiders tend to think of the academic life of a professor as a cerebral existence on a serene campus with none of the pressures of the sharply competitive, real world. In this academic nirvana, the professor shares information with small classes of highly motivated, well-prepared students and writes an occasional article or book on an arcane subject. Faculty life on campus is thus marked not by job-related stress but by collegiality, a leisurely work pace, and successive promotions to full professorship.

Yet many who teach in colleges or universities would probably describe a different picture. They see important academic decisions being made without their knowledge or participation. They see the following: requirements for promotion and tenure that are so stringent as to be largely unrealizable; themselves as prisoners in their jobs with little chance to move up the academic ladder; students in their classes who are inadequately prepared and marginally interested in the subject matter; and institutional expectations that they be good teachers, engage in significant research, actively participate in community and institutional service, and turn in sterling performances in all three areas. For many faculty members, is it any wonder that the outcome is stress?

Exactly what is stress? It can be defined as the body's physical, mental, and chemical reactions to all the things that surround it and impinge on it. Stress can be beneficial if it triggers growth and improves the professor's performance. But it can be destructive if it leads to burnout, alcoholism, tension headaches, irritability, and boredom.

The destructive consequences of faculty stress are not inevitable. They result solely from improperly managing and reacting to stressful events. This volume of *New Directions for Teaching and Learning* spells out the specific causes of faculty stress in the mid 1980s. It offers practical and proven ways of coping with the many stressful situations facing today's professors.

In Chapter One, Robert A. Armour, Rosemary S. Caffarella, Barbara S. Fuhrmann, and Jon F. Wergin discuss academic burnout, a condition that occurs with disturbing frequency and often strikes the most competent and committed faculty. The authors suggest a useful array of institutional responses to burnout and describe the key characteristics inherent in an institutional climate that can counter it. In Chapter Two, I present current research evidence on the causes of academic stress. I cite considerable evidence in the literature to suggest that professors in the 1980s face elevated job stress. In Chapter Three, Walter H. Gmelch describes the results of the National Faculty Stress Research Project. He

1

describes the sources of job-related stress as reported by faculty in eighty doctoral-granting universities and offers specific coping strategies that can be used by institutions to reduce the factors that lead to faculty stress.

In Chapter Four, Judith M. Gappa relates the unique stress part-time faculty experience. She pinpoints the issues contributing to their perception that they are academe's second-class citizens, and she spells out what institutions must do to help change this perception. In Chapter Five, Mary Deane Sorcinelli and Marshall W. Gregory examine the tensions arising from conflicting personal life and career demands. The tensions—which cut across all faculty ranks and disciplines and apply to both men and women—are frequently corrosive. Finding a liveable balance between personal life and career demands is essential to maintain a manageable stress level. The authors also describe alternative strategies to improve this situation. What can faculty do to help themselves diminish job-related stress? What coping mechanisms really work? In Chapter Six, Anthony F. Grasha details short-term coping mechanisms, and James L. Noel discusses long-term coping mechanisms in Chapter Seven. In both chapters, the approach is practical and specific.

In Chapter Eight, James C. Quick describes the preventive actions colleges and universities must take to ensure the health and vitality of both the institution and the individuals within it. Four key preventive actions are presented in detail. In Chapter Nine, Ronald D. Simpson and William K. Jackson introduce the unique approach developed by the University of Georgia to promote professional and personal renewal. Now in its third year, the program can serve as a model for other institutions of higher learning.

We now know a good deal about the nature of faculty stress, its origins and effects, and the steps that can be taken to manage it. While gaps remain in our understanding, we know enough to permit faculty members and institutions to take the necessary steps to manage it. The objective is not to try to escape the effects of stress—for it is an inevitable part of academic life—but rather to channel and control our responses to it.

Peter Seldin
Editor

Peter Seldin is professor of management at Pace University, Pleasantville, New York, and author of a number of well-received books on faculty evaluation and development. The most recent, Changing Practices in Faculty Evaluation: A Critical Assessment and Recommendations for Improvement, *was published by Jossey-Bass in 1984.*

In a broad sense, burnout is the condition of boredom, indifference, and discontent with one's profession.

Academic Burnout: Faculty Responsibility and Institutional Climate

Robert A. Armour, Rosemary S. Caffarella, Barbara S. Fuhrmann, Jon F. Wergin

The professor is habitually late for class and often wonders in midclass why in the world he is teaching this subject to these students—"Do they really care about Emily Dickinson? More important, do I really care?" He finds he is increasingly upset with the way the administration is running the place and finally admits he really does not like the chair, dean, or vice president. He will go to another professional conference only if the dean insists in writing, and will himself write a scholarly piece longer than a letter only on the occasion of a manned landing on Venus. He refuses to sit on another curriculum committee because he has already heard all the arguments for completely revamping the department's offerings, and he thinks that he probably wrote the proposal the last time this was done a decade and a half ago anyway. He no longer even tries to learn the names of new assistant professors, even though he believes they will be running the

P. Seldin (ed.). *Coping with Faculty Stress.*
New Directions for Teaching and Learning, no. 29. San Francisco: Jossey-Bass, Spring 1987.

department within the year. He finds that he cannot wait to get home after class for a couple of glasses of sherry, or beer if sherry is no longer in the budget because his last raise was not what it should have been and his son's orthodontist bill cannot be put off any longer. He begins to take serious interest in the university's early retirement plan and wonders if his long-time hobby of raising orchids could be somehow turned to profit.

This professor, who is found on many college and university campuses, has become one of the most pressing problems facing academe in the last years of the twentieth century. He is suffering from job burnout.

Burnout as Academic Malaise

In a broad sense burnout is the condition of boredom, indifference, and discontent with one's profession. For the faculty, the situation is serious because burnout affects a professor's teaching, research, and service, the three traditional roles of a college or university educator. The sense of detachment can be contagious for students and colleagues.

The phenomenon has often been observed. Schuster and Bowen (1985) report that "at two-thirds of the campuses we visited, faculty morale seemed no better than fair, and at a quarter of the campuses we characterized morale as 'very poor.' . . . Again and again we interviewed senior faculty members who were angry, embittered, and feeling devalued and abandoned." A Carnegie report (Carnegie Foundation for the Advancement of Teaching, 1985) claims that 40 percent of college faculty members are planning to leave the profession within five years.

The popular view is that many senior faculty members, feeling locked into their jobs by a tight job market, bored with teaching the same courses year after year to students who care only about grades and jobs, and undervalued by the administration and society, have lost interest in their work. Because they are tenured, there is little the institution can do except try to control the damage they do. This widely accepted picture of college faculty, however, is challenged by other important studies. Eble and McKeachie (1985), for example, found the 90 percent of the faculty responding to their survey were moderately or well satisfied with their roles as faculty members. In an in-depth study of faculty attitudes at Indiana University, Sorcinelli (1985) found no widespread depression about the profession and uncovered generally good morale among the faculty.

The contradiction among these studies can probably be explained in part by varying assumptions about what burnout means in various populations. In one sense, the term refers to a clinical condition directly related to stress and resulting in an inability to function in the job. Melendez and de Guzman (1983, p. 16) have used this limited psychiatric definition in their monograph: "Burnout in academe is the result of negatively perceived, work-related events or conditions that produce a level of persistent stress resulting in chronic frustration, tiredness or exhaustion, adverse behavior, and inefficiency and/or dysfunction in one's work." This is the stress affecting airline controllers, automobile executives, and prison wardens; but it is likely that only a small percentage of faculty members suffer from the disease. In a broader sense, however, the word has become a cliché to stand for a more common condition in which job dissatisfaction influences job performance. While less precise from a scholarly point of view, this definition has achieved general acceptance and has become the operative meaning for most discussions of faculty morale.

Major Influences on Faculty Stress

Whatever the definition used, it is important to realize that almost all recent studies of the faculty have revealed some level of dissatisfaction serious enough to require concern. The seeds of the problem should be obvious. Most energetic professors reach top rank in the professoriate with another twenty or so years left before retirement. There can be no more promotions and there will be insignificant salary increases. Monotony can be a problem. Rarely, one suspects, is the problem so serious as to cause major clinical job dysfunction, but often dissatisfaction is significant enough to lead to unhappiness, which can affect teaching, research, and service in important ways. The level of dissatisfaction will vary greatly depending on institution and discipline, as Clark (1985) has shown. Other factors such as rank, time in rank, time at the institution, and teaching level also influence the degree of dissatisfaction; gender and race do not seem to be prominent determinants.

While admitting that the extent and nature of burnout will vary from person to person, we have nevertheless been able to identify several major influences on faculty stress in the literature and from our research with the humanities faculty at Virginia Commonwealth University.

Monotony. Faculty members are perhaps in the only profession in which the most qualified people perform the same tasks they did when they entered the profession. In business, when a person moves up the corporate ladder, he or she assumes different responsibilities, but in academe the duties remain much the same.

Lack of Advancement. Once one reaches full professorship, there is no more opportunity for promotion and very slight chance of a move to another institution.

Lack of Conviction. Many faculty members experience a lack of conviction that what they are doing has value. Students seem to value job-related instruction, and society tends to reward efforts that have a

6

tangible outcome, so professors of abstract subjects especially wonder if their work is important.

Lack of Community. Many older faculty members tell us that a sense of community is missing in some institutions of higher education. The demise of the community is complex but was probably caused by the increased emphasis on research and by competition caused by new tenure and promotion guidelines.

Changing Mission. The role of higher education has shifted since most older faculty members entered the profession, and in many institutions faculty members believe that the mission has changed without their consent. For example, the necessity for teaching the marginally prepared student is a laudable goal, but not one many faculty members choose for themselves.

Lack of Leadership. Both society at large and the faculty in particular sense the lack of creative leadership among colleges and universities, often resulting from threats of legal actions and budget restrictions. Many faculty members believe that their institutions are floating along on troubled waters. Their only direction, it sometimes seems, is provided by economic exigency.

Stultifying Reward Structure. When the reward structure no longer motivates, and the institutional climate no longer fosters productivity, professors find that their involvement with the college and its students becomes minimal (see Chapter Three).

Under these circumstances, faculty members must define vitality individually. As faculty members mature and age, their interests will shift, and the sense of being vital must shift at the same time. Senior professors may view themselves as being as vital as ever, but from an institutional perspective, productivity has apparently dropped off. The odds are good that maturing professors will experience a broadening of interest and that their private and family lives will become increasingly important. These new interests will have to be fit into the individual's schedule, and the sense of vitality and productivity will have to be adjusted accordingly.

The literature and our research have shown that most senior faculty members are very good at redefining their roles as they mature. For the most part, they work within the system to establish their own niche. Although they may be angry with students or the administration or bored at times, the faculty members we interviewed have determined their own interests for teaching, research, and service and have convinced the university to accept those interests as fundamental to the institution's mission. Each is making an important contribution to the university and its students and to his or her own life. One devoted her career to teaching with nary a thought to research, another became an expert on seventeenth-century sailing and sailed a replica of an ancient ship across the ocean, another wrote plays in a department that originally emphasized writing for scholarly publications, and so on. Successful faculty members seek out their own interests within the broad needs of the institution.

Since establishing a niche is an individual matter, to be negotiated between the professor and his or her department, the faculty must bear the responsibility for avoiding burnout and maintaining vitality. Most successful careers, however, will develop in an institutional environment that fosters development. Support is important if a faculty member is to have the time and encouragement to develop, and the institution's reward structure must recognize and accept development.

Institutional Responses and Support

In order to describe the type of programs offered by an institution, we have devised a continuum that categorizes different strategies for maintaining faculty vitality. At one end are the simple and inexpensive programs such as grants-in-aid. As one moves along the continuum, the programs become more complex and expensive until one reaches early retirement. The entire continuum is shown in Figure 1. Each of the points on the continuum can be illustrated by numerous activities—some ordinary, others innovative.

Aids in Accomplishing What Is Presently Underway. These are activities that assist professors in accomplishing projects they have already begun. They do not call for important shifts in faculty activity, but they do permit the time or money to improve ongoing projects. Widely used examples of this type of activity include minigrants for research or teaching improvement: course reductions for research, service, or curricular development; travel funds for attending conferences or for research; and retreats. One example of an innovative program that has been especially successful at offering this type of assistance is the career development program at the College of Charleston, in South Carolina. It has made available to its faculty small grants and in-house fellowships and encouraged teaching outside a faculty member's home department. Although some colleges and universities have been more imaginative than others in their approaches to this type of assistance, all colleges we have studied have had some programs that give inexpensive aid to faculty members who can identify short-term, needed projects.

Temporary Change in Responsibilities. These programs permit faculty members to leave their routine responsibilities so that they may refine teaching methods, take on an unusual teaching assignment, or begin new

Figure 1. Continuum of Strategies for Maintaining Faculty Vitality

Aids in accomplishing what is presently underway	Temporary change in responsibilities	Midcareer shifts	Early retirement

research. They provide a break in professional monotony with the expectation that the professor will return to normal duties, although perhaps with new interests. Typical examples include sabbaticals, Fulbright scholarships, the National Faculty Exchange, National Endowment for the Humanities (NEH) summer institutes, and research leaves sponsored by numerous national agencies. Programs that accomplish the same objectives but vary the traditional model include disciplinary seminars held by Stanford University for professors from throughout California and the Faculty Resource Network established by New York University and several New England colleges. Others include Consortium Professorships designed by colleges in central Virginia to permit senior faculty members to help other faculty members design new courses; the University of Kansas Intra-University Visiting Professor Program, which permits professors to teach for a year in a new department; and the Cooperative Program for the Professional Renewal of Faculty (COPROF), a cooperative venture at the Universities of Nebraska and Minnesota that teaches faculty members new methods for career planning and renewal.

Midcareer Shifts. These programs enable a faculty member to make a clear career shift: to leave the normal tasks and take on an entirely new set of responsibilities. Typical midcareer shifts are those in which the professor retrains for a new field, moves to an administrative position, or departs academe and is employed in business or government. Important institutional programs include faculty retraining programs sponsored by colleges and consortia as divergent as J. Sargeant Reynolds Community College, in Richmond, Virginia; Regis College, in Denver, Colorado; Northern Illinois University; and the University of Wisconsin system. Some of these programs retrain faculty for positions inside the institution, whereas others retrain for outside employment.

Early Retirement. In the strictest sense early retirement is not faculty development, because it is designed to move faculty members out of the profession and into retirement or perhaps another career. If to another career, it is akin to the retraining just discussed as a midcareer shift. However, because it is the logical last point on the continuum and because many faculty members plan their career development keeping in mind the idea of leaving the institution before the usual retirement age, it is included here. Early retirement is designed to move higher-paid senior faculty members out of the profession some years before they normally would retire. The institution provides incentives to make early retirement attractive (continuing health insurance, partial salary, use of office space and secretaries, and so on). It gains by being able to hire a lower-salaried junior faculty member in the same position. Most institutions that have tried this program have been delighted with the results, as have the faculty members who have taken advantage of it.

Institutional Climate for Development

A college or university that wishes to counter burnout and encourage maximum faculty vitality and productivity cannot be locked into a single attitude about development. After hours of listening to faculty members talk about their careers and their institutions, we can imagine the ideal college or university climate for encouraging faculty development. The key to developing the senior faculty lies not in an institution's *programs*, but in its *climate*. Although some programs undeniably have an impact on the faculty and some strategies are especially effective, the most valuable contribution an institution can make to the careers of senior faculty members is the creation of a climate receptive to the type of changes they might want to make. Two characteristics of development programs at the ideal institution are the following:

1. It has a broad-based development program. Because faculty needs will vary greatly, developmental options should be various. One value of the continuum just described is that an institution can use it to measure the breadth of its program. At a minimum the institution should have several activities at each point of the continuum. Large numbers of faculty members will probably not engage each option at one time, but a range of options will be essential to satisfy a variety of faculty members.

2. It has diverse programs and activities. Faculty members can make changes in their careers more easily if they have numerous choices on campus. Some campuses clearly lend themselves to diversity more easily than others. But given the limitations of the institution, the more choices of activities the faculty members have, the better. For example, a chance to teach alumni, elderly students, or even advanced high school students in special programs can offer the faculty variety.

Obviously, these programs can require financial resources, equipment, and space beyond the means of most colleges and universities. One solution is to form a consortium of neighboring institutions. Combining activities and facilities and sharing the financial burden may make the projects feasible. The colleges should be close enough to enable the faculty to participate in activities at all member institutions without having to relocate.

We can identify characteristics of our ideal institution that would create the best climate in which faculty members can develop careers that suit them and their institutions. Good faculty members will find their own niche at institutions characterized by qualities ideally found in any decent college or university.

1. The administration and faculty must understand the problems of burnout and be prepared to offer all faculty members the opportunity to discover their individual niches. There must of course be recognition of

the needs of the institution, but both administration and faculty must place individual needs on a par with institutional ones.

2. The institution and the administration must be flexible enough to permit development plans that are not copies of each other and that deviate from the way in which the college has always expected faculty members to operate. Senior faculty members will often go their own way in finding their niche, and the institution must find ways to accommodate eccentricities.

3. The missions of the institution and the department must be broad enough to permit flexibility. If a mission, for example, calls for faculty members to spend 100 percent of their time teaching and serving, a faculty that desires to change by beginning research and writing will be frustrated.

4. Faculty members will feel better about their role and about any changes they make if there is a supportive community. Many faculty members seek a relational group—often within their departments—that gives a sense of belonging and acceptance. Excellent nonthreatening support can often also come from a faculty development office.

5. Faculty members want to be involved in institutional governance, and especially want to have a say in matters that affect their careers. Many faculty members believe that they have lost control of their careers; they will be promoted when the institution is ready, and they will earn whatever salary the dean chooses. Senior faculty members especially, by virtue of their rank and education, want to be consulted on major academic and professional matters.

6. Development is a complex process and most faculty members need assistance in discovering available resources and anticipating how the department will receive their decisions. Knowledgeable and sensitive department chairs are the key to successful faculty development.

7. Faculty members must be assured that they will be rewarded for their career development, even if it takes them into new directions. Obviously, not all career choices can be rewarded equally or in the same manner, but the system of rewards should be flexible enough to recognize the value of activities to the institution and the individual.

If the professor imagined at the beginning of this chapter has developed clinical burnout, there is probably little an institution can do to help. But if the problem is one of boredom, then the professor can be helped if he or she is given the opportunity to find new interests. Burnout, in the nonclinical sense, is a serious problem that can be relieved, if not eliminated, in an institutional climate that encourages good faculty members to continue to grow, explore, and change.

References

Carnegie Foundation for the Advancement of Teaching. "The Faculty: Deeply Troubled." *Change*, 1985, *17* (4), 31–34.

Clark, B. R. "Listening to the Professoriate." *Change*, 1985, *17* (4), 36–43.

Eble, K. E., and McKeachie, W. J. *Improving Undergraduate Education Through Faculty Development: An Analysis of Effective Programs and Practices.* San Francisco: Jossey-Bass, 1985.

Melendez, W. A., and de Guzman, R. M. *Burnout: The New Academic Disease.* ASHE-ERIC Higher Education Research Reports, no. 9. Washington, D.C.: Association for the Study of Higher Education, 1983.

Schuster, J., and Bowen, H. "Public Policy and the Future of the Professoriate." Paper presented at the National Conference of the American Association for Higher Education, Chicago, March 1985.

Sorcinelli, M. D. "Faculty Careers: Personal, Instructional, and Societal Dimensions." Paper presented at the American Educational Research Association Conference, Chicago, March 1985.

All the authors of this chapter are on the staff of Virginia Commonwealth University in Richmond. Robert A. Armour is professor of English and former faculty fellow with the Center for Educational Research and Faculty Resources (CEDR). Rosemary S. Caffarella is associate professor of adult education. Barbara S. Fuhrmann is professor of counselor education and also a fellow with CEDR. Jon F. Wergin is associate professor and associate director of CEDR.

There is evidence in the research literature that the decade of the 80s has been, and is, producing a generation of professors trying to cope with surprisingly high levels of job stress.

Research Findings on Causes of Academic Stress

Peter Seldin

It takes only a few minutes of conversation with college or university professors around the country to realize that academic stress is a national phenomenon. An eastern professor refers to his university as a "stress factory." A midwestern faculty member insists that the words *stress* and *academic* are redundant. A professor at a West Coast university reports that her stress level is several notches higher than it was when she worked in industry. How prevalent and how deep is stress among today's professors?

There is evidence in the literature that the decade of the 1980s has been, and is, producing a generation of professors trying to cope with surprisingly high levels of job stress. Melendez and de Guzman (1983), for example, in a widely discussed survey of almost 2,000 faculty members at 17 colleges, found that 62 percent acknowledged severe or moderate job stress. A similar finding is reported by Gmelch (1984). In a survey of more than 1,900 professors at 80 public and private universities, he found that 60 percent of the total daily stress in their lives came from their work as faculty members.

In the absence of comparative percentages from previous decades, a trend cannot be established, but it is not unreasonable to conclude that the academic environment of the 1980s is such that it imposes considerable stress on professors. There are a number of reasons for this.

P. Seldin (ed.). *Coping with Faculty Stress.*
New Directions for Teaching and Learning, no. 29. San Francisco: Jossey-Bass, Spring 1987.

1. Requirements for promotion and tenure are so stringent today as to be unrealizable for many academics.

2. Academic retrenchment, jobless faculty, inflation, and the changing composition of student bodies are altering the academic environment.

3. Professors are more aware today of the wide discrepancy between their hopes and expectations and the actual rewards offered by their profession.

4. Fewer job-change opportunities are available, and many faculty members see themselves as imprisoned in their jobs with little chance to ascend the academic ladder.

5. Many full-time faculty members perceive part-time faculty members, who are growing in numbers, as a potential job threat.

What are the specific sources of stress among college and university professors? What causes the pressure-cooker frustration they experience as faculty members? Many researchers have devised convenient groupings for producers of stress, and although the groupings tend to vary among researchers, certain categories appear consistently in the literature. These categories are described in the subsequent sections of this chapter.

Inadequate Participation in Institutional Planning and Governance

Faculty members share a widespread belief that their proper share of governance in colleges and universities has eroded. Anderson (1983) and Kamber (1984) report that professors believe that they are less involved now than formerly in the planning and governance of their institutions. The prestigious Carnegie Foundation for the Advancement of Teaching commissioned a nationwide survey that concluded that most faculty members today believe they have very little chance to influence their institutions' policies (Jacobson, 1985).

In another nationwide study involving 5,000 faculty members at 93 colleges and universities, Magarrell (1982) notes a decline in faculty participation in institution planning and governance from 64 percent in 1970 to 44 percent in 1980.

Adams (1980) is persuaded that stress in the workplace inevitably arises when people believe that important decisions or changes directly affecting them are made without their knowledge or participation. It is not surprising that the absence of faculty participation in important academic decision making offers fertile ground for professorial stress.

Too Many Tasks, Too Little Time

One of the most powerful sources of academic stress is excessive demands to perform a wide range of professional and personal tasks within an impossibly short time (Baldwin and Blackburn, 1981; Larkin and Clagett, 1981; Bess, 1982).

It happens with oppressive frequency that professors are expected—as a matter of routine—to manage, and manage successfully, a multiplicity of tasks in a short time. Usual tasks include preparing for classes, keeping current in the discipline, pursuing research, writing journal articles, attending committee meetings, performing community and institutional service, and attending professional conferences.

Assuming the professor is not a hermit, there will also be family obligations as well as the desire to engage in personal activities for relaxation.

The result is often like a juggling act in which some balls fall on the floor. One can fit only so many tasks into a time slot, and the time spent on one task is taken away from another. When considerable time is devoted to preparing a manuscript, scant time is left for class preparation, and almost no time is left for family.

For many faculty members, the inevitable result of daily pressure is frustration and stress. Perhaps this is why more than half of faculty members in a study by Sorcinelli (1985) report a high degree of stress in finding enough time to manage all the various responsibilities of academic life while balancing career with family obligations. In an earlier study, Peters and Mayfield (1982) found that almost 50 percent of faculty members report a high degree of stress in trying to balance teaching load, institutional expectations for research and service, and retaining time for family.

Gmelch (1984), listing the ten leading stress-producers for faculty members, includes several relating to time constraints—feeling overloaded with work, not having sufficient time to keep current in one's discipline, and having little or no time for personal matters. In examining the relative impact of different stressful situations at work, Adams (1980) says that having too much to do and too little time in which to do it tops the list of chronic work-related stress situations.

Low Pay and Poor Working Conditions

A number of researchers cite low pay and poor working conditions as major contributors to faculty stress. Bowen and Schuster (1985) told the annual meeting of the American Association for Higher Education that comparatively low salaries and deteriorating working conditions were fueling faculty anxiety to such a degree that higher education could face a mass exodus of its best teachers. The two researchers noted that the purchasing power of faculty salaries has declined 19 percent in the last fifteen years. And they pointed out that their two-year study of the American professoriate had documented widespread and deep feelings of dissatisfaction among faculty members over low pay and inadequate facilities that are steadily worsening because of deferred maintenance. Such dissatisfactions readily translate into faculty stress.

Similar concerns were found by the Carnegie Foundation (Jacobson, 1985). In a nationwide survey of more than 5,000 professors, the predominant opinion in all faculty ranks was that compensation and working conditions were inadequate. Ernst Benjamin, general secretary of the American Association of University Professors (AAUP), told delegates at the 1985 annual meeting that the chief complaint of professors participating in a recent AAUP survey was lack of equipment and research support. He described the current level of faculty salaries as "awful."

The problem of faculty anxiety and stress over low pay is exacerbated by wide differences in salary across disciplines. Because of the popularity of some fields, the gap in pay continues to widen between faculty members in some of the higher-paid disciplines—such as management and business administration—and the rest of the professoriate. As reported in *The Chronicle of Higher Education* ("In Box," 1985), the average nine-month pay of all faculty members in 1984-85 was $29,700, a gain of 7.3 percent over the previous year. But faculty members in business-related fields enjoyed an average salary of $34,500, an increase of 8.6 percent. This widening gap in pay is eroding faculty morale and producing its own measure of stress.

Inadequate Faculty Recognition and Reward

Numerous research studies on the sources of stress among college and university professors cite inadequate recognition and reward, or a variant, as a major culprit (Adams, 1980; Bender and Blackwell, 1982; Melendez and de Guzman, 1983; Seldin, 1984b; Sorcinelli, 1985).

Under this general heading are included such items as (1) policies and procedures that assess faculty performance, (2) academic atmosphere in which evaluation is conducted, (3) pace of promotion in rank, and (4) who receives and who does not receive merit pay.

A good deal of stress arises from the discrepancy between the relative importance institutions attach to teaching, research, and service and the relative importance the faculty would prefer. Most college and university professors have a high regard for classroom teaching and devote vast amounts of time and effort to it. But the reward system at many institutions places greater value on research and publication than on classroom teaching. When that happens, the result is faculty stress (Peters and Mayfield, 1982). Boyer (1985) underscores the same point when he observes that faculty members are caught in the crossfire of conflicting signals about what their priorities should be. They feel pulled in opposite directions. They are told that classroom teaching is of vital importance, but teachers soon learn from experience that research matters more for promotion and tenure.

To further complicate matters, professors are often unclear as to the expectations of their institution regarding standards of faculty performance in teaching, research, and service (Gmelch, 1984). Too often they are unaware of the criteria their college or university uses to evaluate their performance. This unfamiliarity adds to academic stress. There is also the matter of insufficient feedback on faculty performance. Too often faculty members have no idea how others perceive their performance. The opinions of the department chair and their colleagues remain unarticulated. Because there is little or no feedback, unfavorable tenure or promotion decisions come as a shock to many professors. No one had taken the time or energy to tell them how well or poorly they were doing.

Professors must believe—with justification—that their efforts mean something and will be recognized by their institution (Seldin, 1984a). Unless they believe, it, and the belief is supported by the institution, it is only a matter of time before their motivation and morale sag as their stress levels rise.

Unrealized Career Expectations and Goals

Most professors would probably agree that their reputation rests largely on publications, presentations at professional meetings, and obtaining research grants. They guard their reputations as vigilantly as professionals do in any field. Yet the professor's gut feeling of personal success or failure rests less on the number of publications, paper presentations, and research grants secured than on whether these achievements measure up to the professor's self-expectations and goals.

Gmelch (1984) found that because faculty members impose unusually high expectations on themselves, failure to meet such expectations produced considerable professorial anguish, regardless of discipline. Alexander and others (1983) cite unrealistically high levels of self-expectation and self-imposed pressures for achievement as major contributors to faculty stress.

Even senior faculty members are not immune from the sudden feeling of failure and depression that accompanies a letter of rejection from a journal editor or conference planner (Seldin, 1985). As for junior faculty members who have spent years in graduate school preparing for a teaching career, denial of tenure is a devastating blow. The feeling that one does not measure up is pervasive and powerful. *Stress* is a mild word to sum up the situation.

Unsatisfactory Interactions

Another factor that produces high stress among professors is unsatisfactory interactions with students, faculty colleagues, and department chairs. Melendez and de Guzman (1983) report that student apathy and unwarranted expectation of high grades are a prime source of professorial stress. Considerable stress is also triggered at the time professors evaluate the performance of their students and when students evaluate the teaching performance of their professors. Boyer (1985) finds that many faculty members believe that academic standards have declined and that students today are less interested in learning than preceding generations of students. The Carnegie Foundation for the Advancement of Teaching, in a survey of professors at 310 institutions, reports the predominant faculty view that students should be better prepared before they enter college (Jacobson, 1985). Professors are dismayed at the lack of preparation and resentful about using valuable class time to teach what the students should already know. The by-product is faculty stress.

Perhaps the dominant source of stress from interactions with colleagues is the lack of mutual trust, respect, and rapport among faculty members (Seldin, 1985). When personal chemistry between people is wrong, the stress level rises. It remains high in academic departments that are beset by political divisions, professional jealousies, bickering, and back-biting. Melendez and de Guzman (1983) report that the primary sources of stress related to faculty colleagues are lack of motivation, lack of teamwork, and lack of respect from colleagues. In interactions with department chairs, stress arises from excessive workloads, budgetary constraints, and lack of faculty influence on the chair's decisions. Gmelch (1984) suggests that an additional source of stress is failure to understand how the department chair evaluates faculty performance.

In general, professors do not give high marks to their campus administrators. Boyer (1985), in reporting the results of the nationwide survey conducted by the Carnegie Foundation, says that two-thirds of faculty members rate their administrators as "fair" or "poor." And the same percentage label their administrators as being "somewhat" or "very" autocratic. Interestingly, more than half also believe that when faculty members become administrators they suffer amnesia about what it means to be a teacher and to conduct research. There appear to be inherent irrec-oncilable differences between the demands of the academic administration and the needs of professors. The inherent tension between them translates into faculty stress.

In summary, the research literature suggests that college and university professors are buffeted at work by a number of stress-producing factors. These include

- Inadequate participation in institutional planning and governance
- Too many tasks to do in too little time
- Low pay and poor working conditions
- Inadequate faculty recognition and reward

- Unrealized career expectations and goals
- Unsatisfactory interactions with students, colleagues, and the department chair.

I will personalize research findings in the literature by following a professor in the performance of a typical day's work. We will spare him from the indignity of experiencing all these stress factors in a single day. But, for the sake of realism, he will encounter some of them.

A Day in the Life of Professor Howard Ward

Grading papers until midnight, the professor oversleeps in the morning. Agitated, he realizes he will be late to class again, the third time in as many weeks. He grabs a fast breakfast of scalding coffee and a hard roll and is out the door. He worries about running into the department chair, how to explain his lateness this time, and how to squeeze his sixty-minute classroom lecture into forty-eight minutes.

Arriving on campus, Professor Ward walks briskly to the classroom; more a slow jog than a walk. Only when he is nearly there does he realize that the important notes he needs for the lecture are still in his office. Already late for class, Ward decides he will have to rely on memory and do without the notes, despite their importance to his lecture.

The lecture suffers. Not only does he forget and skip a few important topics, which leaves the lecture disjointed, but his presentation is dispirited. He knows he has done a poor job.

Unfortunately for Ward, so do two senior members of his department, who attended class to observe his teaching performance. On leaving, they say they'll meet with him the next day to discuss their observations and conclusions.

Later, the professor is edgy and almost involuntarily speaks sharply to the department secretary for not getting out his correspondence. Overhearing the brief exchange, the department chair comes out and, in tone of voice and look, reprimands Professor Ward. The secretary was on a special assignment, the department head explains, that had to be completed before anything else.

The day's mail brings the professor the unexpected rejection of a long manuscript that had taken months of work. The editor's note thanks the professor for the submission but advises that two reviewers found it fatally flawed and in their judgment beyond repair.

That afternoon Ward attends an important campus committee meeting. Deep in thought about the rejected manuscript, he fails to recognize a question directed at him by the committee head. Professor Ward would have a better idea of what is going on at the university if he would pay more attention, remarks the committee head. The sarcasm brings furtive smiles to the faces of the other committee members.

20

When the professor arrives home he is tense, irritable, and short-tempered with his boisterous teenagers and his wife. This provokes an argument. He spends hours sitting on the couch alone, alternating between being angry with himself and feeling sorry for himself, until he finally goes to bed for a fitful sleep. Professor Howard Ward is a victim of academic stress.

References

Adams, J. D. *Understanding and Managing Stress: A Workbook in Changing Life Styles.* San Diego, Calif.: University Associates, 1980.

Alexander, L., Adams, R. D., and Martray, C. R. "Personal and Professional Stressors Associated with the Teacher Burnout Phenomenon." Paper presented at the American Educational Research Association, Montreal, Canada, March 1983.

Anderson, R. E. *Higher Education in the 1970s: Preliminary Technical Report for Participating Institutions.* New York: Institute of Higher Education, Teachers College, Columbia University, 1983.

Baldwin, R. G., and Blackburn, R. T. "The Academic Career as a Developmental Process: Implications for Higher Education." *Journal of Higher Education*, 1981, 52, 598–614.

Bender, R. C., and Blackwell, M. W. *Professional Expectations, Stress, and University Faculty: An Analysis.* Houston, Tex.: Southern Association for Counselor Education and Supervision, 1982.

Bess, J. *University Organization: A Matrix Analysis of the Academic Professions.* New York: Human Sciences Press, 1982.

Bowen, H. R., and Schuster, J. H. "Public Policy and the Future of the Professoriate." Paper presented at the American Association for Higher Education Conference, Chicago, March 1985.

Boyer, E. "How Professors See Their Future." *The New York Times*, August 18, 1985, p. 36.

Gmelch, W. H. "Pressures of the Professoriate: Individual and Institutional Coping Strategies." In T. B. Massey (ed.), *Proceedings of the Tenth International Conference on Improving University Teaching.* College Park, Maryland, July 1984.

"In Box" *Chronicle of Higher Education*, January 9, 1985, p. 27.

Jacobson, R. L. "New Carnegie Data Show Faculty Members Uneasy About the State of Academe and Their Own Careers." *Chronicle of Higher Education*, December 18, 1985, p. 1.

Kamber, R. "Dissatisfied Professors and the Erosion of Shared Governance." *Chronicle of Higher Education*, December 12, 1984, p. 96.

Larkin, P., and Clagett, C. *Sources of Faculty Stress and Strategies for Its Management.* Largo, Md.: Office of Institutional Research, Prince Georges Community College, 1981.

Magarrell, J. "Decline of Faculty Morale Laid to Governance Role, Not Salary." *Chronicle of Higher Education*, November 10, 1982, p. 1.

Melendez, W. A., and de Guzman, R. M. *Burnout: The New Academic Disease.* ASHE-ERIC Higher Education Research Reports, no. 9. Washington, D.C.: Association for the Study of Higher Education, 1983.

Peters, D. S., and Mayfield, J. R. "Are There Any Rewards for Teaching?" *Improving College and University Teaching*, 1982, 30 (3), 105–110.

Seldin, P. "In Search of Academic Excellence: An Organizational Perspective." In

T. B. Massey (ed.), *Proceedings of the Tenth International Conference on Improving University Teaching*, College Park, Maryland, July 1984a.

Seldin, P. "Successfully Managing Academic Stress." Paper presented at the National Conference of the Professional and Organizational Development Network, Monterey, California, October 1984b.

Seldin, P. "Academic Stress: Research Findings on Causes." In T. B. Massey (ed.), *Proceedings of the Eleventh International Conference on Improving University Teaching*, Utrecht, The Netherlands, July 1985.

Sorcinelli, M. D. "Faculty Careers: Personal, Institutional, and Societal Dimensions." Paper presented at the American Educational Research Association Conference, Chicago, March 1985.

Peter Seldin is professor of management at Pace University, Pleasantville, New York, and author of a number of well-received books on faculty evaluation and development. The most recent, Changing Practices in Faculty Evaluation: A Critical Assessment and Recommendations for Improvement, *was published by Jossey-Bass in 1984.*

*What is the true nature of faculty stress and what can
institutions of higher education do to help their faculty
members become more productive and healthy?*

What Colleges and
Universities Can Do
About Faculty Stressors

Walter H. Gmelch

Despite its uniqueness and longevity, university teaching remains one of
the most misunderstood occupations in the world. Few have ventured to
study the professoriate, and when exploring its dimensions the discourse
most often remains at the philosophical and esoteric levels. Although
academicians eagerly study other professions, they seldom find the time
and interest to investigate their own. John Gardner has stated that education is to professors as water is to goldfish: They swim in it but never
think to study it.

The issue of faculty stress is becoming increasingly important to
institutions and faculties of higher education. This chapter focuses on
institutional strategies for coping with stress. The faculty stress cycle will
be introduced to guide the reader through the discussion and explain the
framework used to undertake a comprehensive study of faculty stress. Next,
the results of the National Faculty Stress Research Project will be reviewed
to provide an understanding of the pressures of the professoriate, in terms
of both individual stressors and general factors of stress. Finally, the
research findings will be applied to institutional coping strategies.

P. Seldin (ed.). *Coping with Faculty Stress.*
New Directions for Teaching and Learning, no. 29. San Francisco: Jossey-Bass, Spring 1987.

The Typical Faculty Stress Cycle

Stress is a complicated phenomenon subject to a range of definitions. This chapter reflects the four-stage stress cycle depicted in Figure 1. This process begins with Stage I, a set of specific demands, or *stressors*. Excessive meetings, interruptions, and confrontations produce some stress, but how much depends on Stage II, the individual's *perception* of the demand. If the individual does not have the physical or mental resources to meet the demand, he or she perceives that demand as a stressor. The stress created by this discrepancy between demand and personal resources results in a stress *response*—Stage III—taking the form of social, physical, attitudinal, and other reactions. The fourth and final stage, termed *consequences*, pertains to the intensity and long-range negative effects of stress.

Consistent with the stress cycle, I suggest the following definition of stress: one's anticipation of his or her inability to respond (Stage III) adequately to a perceived (Stage II) demand (Stage I), accompanied by the anticipation of negative consequences (Stage IV) due to an inadequate response. The intent of this chapter is to focus on the first, second, and third stages of the stress cycle by identifying faculty members' perceptions of their stressors, and then to provide strategies for how they can respond positively. If the stressors can be identified, the perceptions turned into positive assessments, and the responses used in a variety of ways, then the consequence can be a healthy and productive faculty member.

A National Perspective on the Pressures of the Professoriate

The National Faculty Stress Research Project was undertaken to fulfill the following specific objectives: (1) identify job situations perceived by the faculty as most stressful; (2) group these stressful job situations into interpretable factors; (3) search for significant relationships between perceived stress and personal and professional factors such as academic discipline, rank, tenure, age, and gender; and (4) identify strategies for faculty to cope with stress (Gmelch and others, 1984). It is not the intent of this chapter to recapitulate all our research findings but to extrapolate from the data findings applicable to individuals and institutions for reducing unproductive stress. A brief summary of the methodology, the findings, and the applications follows.

Methodology. From among 184 doctoral-granting universities in the United States, a sample of forty public and forty private universities was randomly selected. Faculty members were stratified by Biglan's (1973) eight clusters of academic disciplines and by academic rank (assistant, associate, and full professor). A sample of 1,920 faculty members was drawn from this stratification, consisting of an equal number of faculty members at public and private universities; equal proportions of assistant, associate, and full professors; and equal proportions of the faculty from

Figure 1. The Stress Cycle

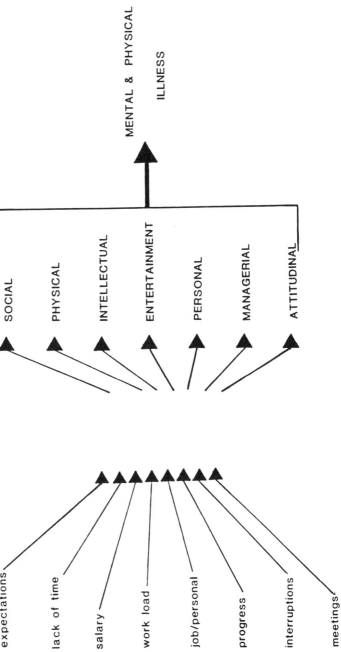

I
STRESSORS

II
PERCEPTIONS

III
RESPONSES

IV
CONSEQUENCES

expectations
lack of time
salary
work load
job/personal
progress
interruptions
meetings

SOCIAL
PHYSICAL
INTELLECTUAL
ENTERTAINMENT
PERSONAL
MANAGERIAL
ATTITUDINAL

MENTAL & PHYSICAL
ILLNESS

each of the eight Biglan disciplinary clusters. The questionnaire developed to measure sources of faculty stress evolved through a series of iterations designed to ensure that all potentially relevant facets of job-related stress were explored. After field testing, the final forty-five item Faculty Stress Index (FSI) was mailed to 1,920 faculty members, with a response rate of 75 percent.

Findings. Overall, faculty reported that 60 percent of the total stress in their lives came from their work. More specifically, we found that of the forty-five stressors, the ten most troublesome were (1) imposing excessively high self-expectations, (2) securing financial support for research, (3) having insufficient time to keep abreast with current events in one's field, (4) low pay for work done, (5) striving for publication of one's research, (6) feeling that one is continually overloaded with work, (7) job demands interfering with personal activities, (8) lack of progress in career, (9) interruptions from telephone and drop-in visitors, and (10) meetings (Gmelch and others, 1984).

When faculty stressors were compared within disciplinary groupings, far more similarities than differences existed in the way the faculty across academia viewed sources of work-related stress. There was strong evidence that the problem of stress in university settings is a general one, common to all disciplines rather than specific to a few disciplines. Also, faculty in a diverse range of disciplines reported similar degrees of stress associated with teaching, research, and service. Of these three major faculty functions, teaching was designated as the most stressful activity.

Next, the multidimensionality of the FSI was investigated through the use of a principal components, varimax solution factor analysis (Gmelch and others, 1984). The results of the factor analysis indicated the presence of five distinct factors that, in combination, accounted for 86 percent of the common variance and included thirty-one stress items with loadings of .40 and above.

Reward and Recognition. The first factor, accounting for over 55 percent of the common variance, addresses the area of faculty rewards and recognition. All eight items deal with inadequate rewards, insufficient recognition, and unclear expectations in all three areas of faculty responsibility: teaching, research, and service.

Time Constraints. The second factor, accounting for about 12 percent of the common variance, reflects time constraints that confront faculty members—insufficient time to keep abreast of current developments, inadequate time for class preparation, interruptions from telephones and drop-in visitors, writing memos and letters, attending meetings, too heavy a work load, and job demands interfering with personal activities. It is interesting to note that none of these stressors relate directly to teaching, research, or service but represent the means, not the ends, of faculty productivity.

Departmental Influence. The third factor, accounting for 7 percent of the common variance, deals with attempts to influence the chair's decisions, resolving differences with the chair, understanding how the chair evaluates faculty performance, and the overall lack of impact on departmental and institutional decision making.

Professional Identity. If one assumes that faculty reputation is built on publications, presentations to conferences, grants, research, and the like, the emergence of the professional identity factor, accounting for 6 percent of the common variance, is not surprising. Add to this factor the item of imposing excessively high self-expectations (the highest stressor for all faculty) and this factor could be the foundation of faculty stress. It is not so much the absolute amount of success faculty members have achieved in publications and research but the relationship between the level of achievement and their personal expectations or aspirations that causes stress. The professor is unique in setting his or her own goals.

Student Interaction. The final factor, accounting for 6 percent of the common variance, relates to the interaction between students and faculty. The faculty members find themselves in conflict over evaluation, advising, and teaching.

With respect to personal and professional differences among the previous five factors, stress universally declined with tenure and as one moved to higher academic ranks of associate and full professor. Differences were also found in the third professional characteristic, discipline, only with respect to rewards and recognition and student interaction.

In the area of personal characteristics—age, gender, and marital status—significant differences were found in two of the five factors: time constraints and professional identity. As faculty age increases, less stress is experienced from these two factors. Married women were identified as having the most stress, and single women experienced the next highest level.

Much like Blackburn's nine assertions about academic careers (1979), our research leads us to some truisms about academic stress.

1. Faculty stress is predictable, depending on age, gender, and marital status.
2. Faculty stress is consistently influenced by the professional variables of tenure and rank.
3. Faculty stress is determined to a high degree by the institutional reward structure.
4. Faculty stress is influenced by time constraints impeding the way to productivity.
5. Faculty stress is influenced by the perceptions of one's own expectations.
6. Faculty stress is universal across all academic disciplines.

Coping Strategies

The following propositions on coping are asserted as a basis for this section of the chapter:

1. The individual is the most important variable; no single coping technique is effective for all individuals in all situations.

2. Individuals cannot change the world around them, but they can change how they relate to it.

3. Coping techniques must be sensitive to cultural, social psychological, and environmental differences in individuals.

4. Individuals who cope best develop a repertoire of techniques to counteract different stressors in different situations.

5. An individual's repertoire of techniques should represent a holistic approach to coping, including known effective strategies such as physical activity, occupational skills, social support, personal hobbies, entertainment, intellectual stimulation, and supportive attitudes (Gmelch, 1984; see also Chapters Six and Seven).

What is the nature of coping? Is there a definitive strategy that institutions can use to help the faculty systematically address the stresses in higher education?

Although disciplines within universities potentially represent different sources of stress, faculty members seem to have more similarities than differences across disciplines. It seems likely, therefore, that institutional strategies for stress management may be applicable across campuses. A caution, however, is noted: A doctor who knows the cure for many illnesses still cannot precisely prescribe the cure for a particular patient until a careful diagnosis is completed. Examination must also be made within specific university settings before accurate prescriptions can be issued. Given this limitation, I suggest generic strategies for coping with the factors of faculty stress.

Stress Factor 1: Reward and Recognition. With respect to insufficient and unclear rewards, goal-setting sessions should be undertaken by department chairs and deans to help faculty members focus on the most productive activities. At a minimum, an annual meeting should be established to address rewarded activities for the next year in teaching, research, and service. Every member should not be expected to produce excellence in each of the three areas every year, but possibly excellence in one and competence in the others. In this way the established goals can also be discussed in relation to their congruence with departmental and university missions such that each faculty member, when combined with the faculty as a whole, represents a faculty productivity portfolio of excellence. Each is then rewarded for his or her contribution to the portfolio.

Recognition has traditionally been viewed as monetary reward for excellence. However, numerous other mechanisms present powerful alternatives to financial benefit. The use of news releases on faculty activities; departmental bulletin boards displaying recent publications; and yearly faculty excellence awards in teaching, service, and research could be bestowed at the departmental level to ensure a more realistic recognition of many deserving faculty members rather than the usual one member of the university at large singled out for excellence.

Stress Factor 2: Time Constraints. Paperwork, meetings, and interruptions represent not ends of academic productivity but the means to goal accomplishment. Faculty members should spring these stress-traps so that they can effectively use their time to achieve their goals. In-service training in time-management techniques may provide the logical remedy, not necessarily to train faculty members in new ideas but to remind them of techniques already known and in need of more consistent practice.

It is particularly ironic that institutions of higher education often ignore their most important resource or treat them as self-sufficient once the Ph.D. is achieved. Faculty development programs addressing such needs as time management can provide a great boost to both faculty morale and productivity. A few of the basic time-management principles that should be reinforced are the following:

1. Assist faculty members in indentifying high pay-off (HIPOs) activities that will help them attain excellence in the crucial products of teaching, research, and service.

2. In the same sense, reduce faculty involvement in less meaningful, low pay-off (LOPOs) processes by cutting back excessive meetings, committee work, and general "administrative" (paperwork).

3. Provide faculty members with a more efficient working environment so that routine paperwork can be dictated through a central dictaphone system or typed into a central wordprocessing pool; telephone calls can be screened so that faculty members can block uninterruptable productive time; and, if possible, faculty members can retreat to a HIPO hideout (workroom) for class preparation, manuscript or grant preparation, and other activities that require quiet, uninterrupted time.

4. Assist faculty members in developing effective self-management techniques, particularly in planning and organization, so that the productive tasks are accomplished.

Stress Factor 3: Departmental Influence. This factor supports numerous studies that reveal that faculty members blame many of their dissatisfactions on the institution's internal structure (McGee, 1971) and their own limited involvement in planning and governance. Although departmental influences are among the most important features of faculty life (Nance, 1981; Cares and Blackburn, 1978), institutions of higher education should not lose sight of the fact that faculty want to influence decisions that affect them but do not desire a total participatory structure riddled with more committees and meetings. Before the level of faculty involvement is determined, chairs and deans should consider the range of appropriate approaches for their faculty, from "raise the issue and let the group decide" to "make the decision independently and then announce it to the faculty." Faculty participation should be decided based on the following criteria: (1) Does the issue under consideration make a difference to the faculty? (2) Does the administrator have adequate information to make a decision without faculty input? (3) Is there goal congruence between administrative and faculty desires?

Stress Factor 4: Professional Identity. Many have postulated that the feeling of being productive is dependent on the relationship between one's achievement and one's level of aspiration, not on absolute productivity (Lewin and others, 1944; March and Simon, 1958). It is crucial, therefore, that faculty members have an opportunity to realistically set goals with the assistance of department chairs and deans. As indicated earlier, the primary cause of stress is excessively high self-expectations. If deans and chairs can help the faculty set a realistic agenda, not only will productivity be focused, but faculty members will also be more satisfied with their accomplishments.

Because younger faculty members, especially women, represent groups suffering most from professional identity stress, support networks and mentoring systems should be provided to give the guidance and collegial support needed to gain understanding and acceptance of one's contribution to his or her profession.

Stress Factor 5: Student Interaction. Much of the stress involved in student interaction stems from its confrontation and conflict orientation. Training in counseling and negotiation skills is most important here. This training should not necessarily focus on soft negotiation skills, such as "how to become friends," or on hard techniques, such as " how to live with adversaries," but on the practices of principled negotiations in which both faculty members and students become problem-solvers seeking wise outcomes efficiently and amicably (Fisher and Ury, 1981).

Concluding Suggestions for Action

The majority of top faculty stressors identified in our research relate directly to time pressures, resource constraints, reward structure, personal identity, and interaction with student and administrators. Some stressors are clearly more controllable than others. Most faculty members and administrators would agree that although they can become better time and interpersonal relations managers, it is more difficult to have an impact on resources and reward structures. However, even in these more difficult areas, the effort is still worthwhile because much of the stress faculty members experience might be alleviated by institutional changes and reappraisal of individual faculty members' capabilities and limitations.

The institutional intervention strategies presented in this chapter represent actions universities and faculty members can take to reduce unproductive tension. Take these suggestions as a starting point toward a future of higher faculty productivity, satisfaction, and health. The actual answers rest with the actions of each faculty member, department, and institution of higher education.

References

Biglan, A. "Relationships Between Subject-Matter Characteristics and the Structure and Output of University Departments." *Journal of Applied Psychology*, 1973, *57*, 204–213.
Blackburn, R. T., and Havighurst, R. J. "Career Patterns of Male Academic Social Scientists." *Higher Education*, 1979, *8*, 5.
Cares, R. C., and Blackburn, R. T. "Faculty Self-Actualization: Factors Affecting Career Success." *Research in Higher Education*, 1978, *7*, 123–136.
Fisher, R., and Ury, W. *Getting to Yes: Negotiating Agreement Without Giving In.* Boston: Houghton Mifflin, 1981.
Gmelch, W. H. "Educators' Response to Stress: Toward a Coping Taxonomy." Paper presented at the American Educational Research Association Conference, New Orleans, April 1, 1984.
Gmelch, W. H., Lovrich, N. P., and Wilke, P. K. "Stress in Academe: A National Perspective." *Research in Higher Education*, 1984, *20*, 477–499.
Lewin, K., Dembo, T., Festinger, L., and Sears, P. S. "Level of Aspiration." In J. M. Hunt (ed.), *Personality and the Behavior Disorders.* New York: Ronald Press, 1944.
McGee, R. *Academic Janus: The Private College and Its Faculty.* San Francisco: Jossey-Bass, 1971.
March, J. G., and Simon, H. A., with Guetzkow, H. *Organizations.* New York: Wiley, 1958.
Nance, E. C. *Self-Investment Theory and Academic Work.* Washington, D.C.: University Press of America, 1981.

Walter H. Gmelch is associate dean for research and field services and professor of educational administration at the College of Education, Washington State University. He has had extensive experience as a business executive, trainer, and consultant.

Part-time faculty members strongly believe that institutional employment policies and practices are developed for the primary benefit of the employer and contribute significantly to the job-related stress they experience.

The Stress-Producing Working Conditions of Part-Time Faculty

Judith M. Gappa

Nearly a third of all faculty members teaching in American colleges and universities today do so on a part-time basis (Gappa, 1984a). They engage in 28 percent of all undergraduate instruction and 21 percent of all graduate-level work (Leslie and others, 1982). The majority of American students will be taught by part-time faculty members at some point during their college education. Thus, status, job satisfaction, and especially the teaching performance of part-time faculty members are matters of great concern to everyone who worries about quality in higher education.

Despite their growing numbers and importance, part-time faculty members are employed under institutional policies and practices that do not take into account the differences among them and tend to reinforce their perception that they are academe's second-class citizens. Part-time faculty members find themselves in a two-tiered system in which the preeminence of tenured faculty members influences most aspects of their working conditions. For many, this situation causes destructive work-related stress.

The part-time faculty members who experience this stress most acutely are those who have the requisite credentials in their academic disciplines and are hopeful of attaining tenure-track status. However, other

P. Seldin (ed.). *Coping with Faculty Stress.*
New Directions for Teaching and Learning, no. 29. San Francisco: Jossey-Bass, Spring 1987.

categories of part-time faculty members are also affected by the stressful nature of their employment. These faculty members teach part-time for a variety of personal and professional reasons. They teach because they have a particular skill, talent, or expertise that is not needed on a full-time basis and because they enjoy the status and stimulation that teaching in a college or university gives them, whether or not they have another career (Gappa, 1984b; Kekke, 1983; Williams and Johansen, 1985). Part-time faculty members who want to teach and do so continuously if work is available are the focus of this chapter. Graduate students teaching part-time while earning degrees and part-time faculty members hired on a contingency basis experience different kinds of stress that are beyond the scope of this chapter.

In varying degrees, continuing part-time faculty members are committed to their institutions and see their work as important. The quality of their professional lives is enhanced to the degree that they experience satisfaction rather than stress. Yet, as this chapter will show, part-time faculty members strongly believe that institutional employment policies and practices are developed for the primary benefit of the employer and contribute significantly to the job-related stress they experience. In conversations with them, and in their writing, they express anger, frustration, and resentment at the lack of value or appreciation given their work; their second-class status in academe; their low earning power, which seems to them unlikely to improve; and the uncertainty and anxiety generated by the temporary nature of their work.

Stress-Producing Working Conditions

As a university administrator responsible for reviewing faculty personnel recommendations, I have frequent conversations with part-time faculty members. They frequently discuss stress-producing aspects of their work, and it is obvious that they do not experience stress in only one or two job-related contexts; they experience it in virtually all aspects of their work as part-time faculty members.

Second-Class Status. Each person occupies a unique social status within a group in an organization. Perception of incongruence between the actual and the potential status causes stress (Quick and Quick, 1984). Granting tenure is the mode of admission to the university association. Teaching staff without tenure do not have the status of members of the university; they are its employees. As such, they experience stress produced by status incongruence (Melendez and de Guzman, 1983).

Part-time faculty members perceive themselves (correctly) as having second-class status. The effects of this status on self-esteem have been articulated by those with whom I have spoken:

> I began to believe that if I were really good, I'd get out of here and get a tenure-track job. Therefore, I must not be that good.

I am just as good as my tenured colleagues but the system
wants cheap labor. The system exploits me. I am better and
deserve better, but there is no hope.

Their perceptions of their status are frequently derived from and reinforced
by their interactions with tenured colleagues. One part-time faculty
member discussed a temporary colleague in her department who had
earned a Ph.D. from Harvard University. She told me that the tenured
faculty of the department find it difficult to recognize and accept the fact
that he possesses this doctoral degree because their stereotype of temporary
faculty members as less well qualified overrides the reality of his
prestigious Ph.D.

Absence of Participation in Decision Making. The absence of participation in decision making is a potent source of stress, especially when
the decision relates to the responsibilities of individuals. Stress is most
acute when the decision is imposed arbitrarily (Warshaw, 1979). Part-time
faculty members are essentially disenfranchised persons in academic governance. Most find few avenues through which they can exercise formal or
informal influence over departmental or institutional decisions that affect
them most directly.

I was shocked to find out how little the departments in
which I taught [as a part-timer] cared about the quality of
my work and how little supervision or administrative support I received, and how reluctant department members were
to have anything to do with me. I was, after all, not a colleague. . . . Exploitative? Like More's Utopia, English
departments offer those lucky few tenured and tenure-track
members full citizenship in an ideal community. Here equal
citizens share the work and the rewards. Like Utopia, however, the ideal contemplative realm of the English department is supported by a group of noncitizens who perform
the work too demeaning and dirty for the citizens to consider. Part-time . . . instructors are not franchised in decision
making. They generally have no voice in departmental policy and are employed in ways that prevent them from moving into citizenship in the departments in which they serve
[Staples, 1984, pp. 3, 5].

Faculty members relate best to each other as equals on an informal
level. Communal efforts and support are important aspects of professionalism (Melendez and de Guzman, 1983). Yet department meetings are scheduled at the tenured faculty's convenience, and committees usually do not
include part-time faculty members, even when they are making decisions

about basic courses these faculty members most often teach (Wilson, 1984). This situation varies little among types of institutions, although there is a greater tendency for part-time faculty members to be more involved in departmental decision-making in community and liberal arts colleges (Gappa, 1984b). Forty-one percent of part-time faculty members surveyed by Abel (1984) were "dissatisfied" or "very dissatisfied" with their participation in departmental or campus governance, and 25 percent indicated similar levels of dissatisfaction with the level of respect they received from the tenured faculty.

Participation in the institution's affairs is directly linked to institutional employment practices. Part-time faculty members are overlooked in decision making and governance because no one, including themselves, knows their length of stay. Vital communication and collegial interactions are limited in part by the unwillingness of tenured faculty members to build bonds that are easily destroyed by falling enrollments or other exigencies.

Inadequate Compensation. Part-time faculty pay per course is usually one-half to four-fifths the amount of a similar class taught by full-time faculty members on an annual salary, regardless of the method of compensation used (Gappa, 1984b). A study of faculty salaries in the California community colleges in 1982–83 showed that part-time faculty members were paid an average of $21.74 per contact hour as compared to $25.69 for full-time faculty members working on overload, and $56.48 for full-time salaried faculty. This amounts to a difference of nearly 260 percent between part-time and full-time faculty members (California State Postsecondary Education Commission, 1983a).

Part-time faculty members frequently do not have built-in cost-of-living increases for length of service. Since full-time faculty members do receive such increments, part-time faculty members who retain their positions are likely to fall further behind their full-time counterparts over time even if they were hired at equivalent salary rates (Gappa, 1984a). Furthermore, most part-time faculty members who work less than half-time do not receive fringe benefits (Gappa, 1984b). Not surprisingly, Abel (1984) found that 79 percent of the part-time faculty members surveyed expressed dissatisfaction with their medical benefits.

Frustration over salary discrepancies increases with the number of years of teaching. One part-time faculty member pointed out that she should be earning the highest salary of her career, yet after eleven years of teaching her actual earning power is declining. Taking inflation into account, she is earning less than she did when she started teaching.

Other part-time faculty members noted the lack of merit salary increases. One had been teaching five years without a salary increase. She was afraid to discuss the subject with her department chair because, with a surplus of well-qualified people available, her dissatisfaction with her salary could lead to her dismissal.

The problem of inadequate compensation is compounded by the lack of rewards and incentives. In Abel's (1984) survey, 47 percent of part-time faculty members were "dissatisfied" or "very dissatisfied" with their salary, and 70 percent were "dissatisfied" or "very dissatisfied" with their opportunities for step and rank increases. The new part-time faculty member full of determination and ambition is quickly disillusioned by the minimal rewards offered for teaching excellence. He or she realizes that quality makes little difference (Wilson, 1984). One part-time faculty member stated, "Our only reward is to be rehired."

Inadequate Performance Evaluation. Decisions regarding work load, assignment, retention, and salary are normally based on formal performance evaluations, but this is rare for part-time faculty members. For them, these decisions are based on enrollment, the need to guarantee tenured faculty work loads, informal personal contacts, availability to teach at certain times, and some evidence of teaching skill (Gappa, 1984b).

When employees do not know the goals and objectives of the job and organization, or on what basis they are evaluated, they experience what Brief and others (1981) label *role ambiguity.* Role ambiguity causes stress because it creates uncertainty about how to be productive, how to improve, and what is rewarded in the organization. Part-time faculty members complain about the lack of formal performance evaluation procedures. One part-time faculty member was upset over the unclear procedures for tenure-track hiring. He believed these decisions were based on politics, affirmative action, and choosing whom "they" please. He expressed a feeling of helplessness about the absence of evaluation systems that could lead to career progression, which stand in contrast to the tenure system of promotion. He asserted that administrators did not want the accountability that would accompany a formal part-time faculty appraisal system. Such an evaluation system would have an impact on their autonomy and flexibility in temporary faculty hiring.

The part-time faculty members with whom I spoke want formal evaluation systems with decisions made, at least in part, on the basis of these evaluations. As one instructor said, "I've been here for nine years. I want my history to count." Another found it amazing that institutions do not bother to monitor their numerous part-time faculty members.

Last Preference in Work Load and Assignment. An immediate and overriding concern of part-time faculty members is their work load and assignment. They returned to this topic repeatedly in our conversations, discussing the numbers and levels of courses they were assigned and the numbers of students in each course. In no other aspect of their employment are the daily reminders of their second-class citizenship and the favored treatment of the tenured and tenure-track faculty so evident.

Part-time faculty members largely teach high-enrollment, lower-division courses (Gappa, 1984b). These courses often have fifty to sixty students per section. The part-time faculty members with whom I spoke all stated how important it is to them to be good teachers. They exhibited commitment to excellence as teachers, and said that they would not "put up with part-time status otherwise." They care about their students, the materials they use, and the quality of their teaching. They experience anxiety when they teach large undergraduate courses and have insufficient time for preparation, individual advising, and development of materials and syllabi.

According to work load formulas for the California State University system, a full-time load for the tenured faculty is four courses; but a full-time load for the temporary faculty is five courses. This is due to the difference between the two groups in departmental and other assignments. These work load formulas also take into account the size, level, and type of course taught. Part-time faculty members observe that, because they are teaching large introductory courses rather than smaller upper-division or graduate courses, they are reducing tenured faculty work loads.

Part-time faculty members also feel exploited because their employment hinges on the need to ensure tenured faculty work loads first, and because it is informal practice to give the tenured faculty preference in schedules and courses. Fully qualified part-time faculty members who seek tenure-track positions resent the fact that they receive little consideration in course assignments, and they wish they could teach courses reflecting both the breadth and depth of their knowledge. Also, they resent that when they serve on departmental committees, supervise graduate students, perform research, or develop new courses, they do so as volunteers because they are usually not compensated for these additional activities.

Job Insecurity. Tenure-track faculty members are given appropriate notice regarding their contract status; their contracts do not simply expire. In contrast, part-time faculty members have no right to assume that their contracts will be renewed even if they perform well because their reappointment is based on enrollment, not excellence. It is common practice to give part-time faculty members no notice and no reason for dismissal (Gappa, 1984a).

A particularly harsh example of the tenuous nature of part-time employment occurred in the California Community College system. After severe budget cuts, 87 percent of the community colleges surveyed reduced their part-time faculty during 1982–83. Forty percent of these colleges reduced part-time faculty through layoffs, 21 percent through attrition, and 27 percent through a combination of the two. In contrast, only 5 percent of the colleges laid off full-time faculty members, and 56 percent reduced full-time faculty through attrition (California State Postsecondary Education Commission, 1983b). The California example underscores what part-time faculty members have long known—that the primary feature of their status in higher education is their expendability. In Abel's (1984) survey, 81 percent of the respondents were "dissatisfied" or "very dissatisfied" with the security of their employment.

Vulnerability to termination is a significant cause of work-related stress. This stress is heightened when the prospect of termination is coupled with few or no prospects of alternative employment (Quick and Quick, 1984). Most part-time faculty members educated for and committed to academic careers find themselves in a saturated market as they emerge from lengthy Ph.D. programs. They are not likely to find a similar position in another organization when they are terminated from a part-time position. They face a nationwide lack of jobs, a highly competitive environment for the few positions that are available, and the need to scavenge for piecemeal work or seek alternative careers. One part-time faculty member stated her dilemma succinctly: "I am thirty-three years old. When we get to the 1990s and the present faculty begin to retire, I won't be a fresh Ph.D. There is no guarantee that I will get equal consideration." She described her frustration over the fact that her primary assignment in teaching is probably detrimental to her chances for a tenure-track position. Now she lacks the time and money to produce scholarship, even though she knows research and publication, rather than teaching performance, will probably be the most important criteria in future tenure-track hiring. As career dreams are shattered, the permanent condition of uncertainty about continuing appointments produces a great deal of stress.

Semester-by-semester appointments based on enrollment mean that part-time faculty members cannot make plans or prepare their courses ahead of time. During the summers they have no written guarantee of appointment, although they may have verbal assurances. Without a guarantee of employment, one continuously reappointed part-time faculty member found he had to pay for his medical benefits over the summer months. Part-time faculty members also often find it difficult to claim unemployment compensation as their institutions argue that there is reasonable assurance of reappointment. This situation puts them in a double bind: They do not have firm offers of employment, but they are not eligible to receive unemployment compensation.

Part-time faculty members usually receive their contract several weeks before the beginning of the semester. However, as semesters begin, there may be fluctuations in enrollment leading to cancellation or changes in classes. Sixty-five percent of those surveyed by Abel (1984) were dissatisfied with the notification time for appointments to teach.

Reducing Stress: What Institutions Can Do

There has been a steady increase in recent decades in the numbers of part-time faculty members employed in all sectors of American higher education. This situation is not likely to change soon. On the contrary, it is more likely that adequately trained and skilled part-time faculty members will be in greater demand and that individuals with advanced degrees who have little opportunity for a traditional academic career may increasingly seek opportunities to teach part-time *if this employment provides sufficient rewards, incentives, and personal satisfaction* (Gappa, 1984a).

There is abundant evidence that employment as a part-time faculty member in higher education is stressful. As a result, part-time faculty members experience unproductive and unhealthy anger, frustration, resentment, and a sense of hopelessness. It is time for institutions of higher education to recognize the valuable contributions that these faculty members make and to change their policies and practices accordingly. If reduction of stress and improved working conditions are to be achieved, centralized responsibility for the employment of part-time faculty members is essential. Free-wheeling departmental autonomy (with attendant abuses) must be replaced by central responsibility for part-time faculty employment to ensure fair and humane treatment.

Current studies of part-time faculty members highlight the differences among them (Gappa, 1984b). Therefore, employment policies and practices must be flexible, taking into account the differences between part-time faculty members in their qualifications, the functions they perform, and their contributions to the institution's objectives. Clearly articulated, humane, and equitable policies and practices based on knowledge of the differences among these faculty members are essential.

The right to tenure is not a right to exploitation of nontenured faculty. Tenured faculty members must realize that it is in their best interest to view part-time faculty members as colleagues, allow them a role in decision making, provide them with reasonable schedules and assignments, and accept them as talented and capable people. The current polarization between full-time tenured faculty members and part-time temporary faculty members should be replaced with the view that all types of faculty perform valued services. Faculty employment should become a continuum rather than a two-tiered system. This continuum should embrace the entire instructional staff from tenured faculty members to fully qualified continuing part-time faculty members committed to their teaching careers to contingency faculty hired to meet enrollment demands. Employees and institutions will be better served when different employment policies are established for different categories of part-time faculty members (Gappa, 1984a).

Stress theorists propose institutional strategies for stress management that seek to eliminate, ameliorate, or change stress-producing factors in jobs. If stress reduction and increased productivity are the goals, institutions of higher education must examine the effects of their policies and practices on part-time faculty members and make improvements. The following suggestions should be considered:

1. Emphasize integrating full- and part-time faculty members and give part-time faculty members a sense of worth and belonging. Their inclusion in faculty governance and departmental deliberations with regard to curricula, courses, teaching materials, and scheduling is imperative.

2. Provide an equitable compensation structure based on qualifications, assignment, and performance that allows for cost-of-living increases, fringe benefits, and career advancement opportunities.

3. Develop an evaluation system aimed at improving teaching effectiveness that articulates clear standards of performance as one basis for decisions about reappointment, assignment, and compensation.

4. Provide increased opportunities to teach a broader spectrum of courses and participate more actively in departmental affairs.

5. Provide an appropriate degree of job security for different categories of part-time faculty members with thoughtful treatment of their interests in renewal, retrenchment, and dismissal decisions.

Most of the preceding suggestions can be accomplished with little, if any, increase in current expenditures for part-time faculty members. These are primarily suggestions for improving the working environment. Improved salaries and benefits for some categories of part-time faculty members could well be worth the additional cost in terms of the resulting increase in productivity.

I asked part-time faculty members with whom I spoke: "What do you want?" They responded that they want (1) part-time work that is well paid and more secure; (2) more choices, options, and flexibility in their teaching assignments; (3) opportunities for advancement; and (4) respect and recognition for the work they do. These are not unreasonable requests. Many part-timers may fairly be characterized as the reluctant victims of a system that exploits them. Personal rather than professional considerations restrict some to part-time work. For many, however, market conditions leave them little choice. They persist in part-time status and teach an increasingly large share of courses because they want to teach and, in turn, colleges and universities want them to teach. Thus, it is in everyone's best interest that employment policies and practices reduce the stress part-time faculty members currently experience and provide them with opportunities for a satisfying teaching career whether or not it is in combination with other careers. The goal must be to enhance rather than discourage their teaching performance and contributions to their institutions.

References

Abel, E. K. *Terminal Degrees: The Job Crisis in Higher Education.* New York: Praeger, 1984.
Brief, A. P., Schuler, R. S., and Van Sell, M. *Managing Job Stress.* Boston: Little, Brown, 1981.

42

California State Postsecondary Education Commission. *Faculty Salaries in the California Community Colleges: 1982–83 Academic Year.* Sacramento: California State Postsecondary Education Commission, 1983a. (ED 234 856)

California State Postsecondary Education Commission. *Impact of 1982–83 Budget Constraints on the California Community Colleges: Commission Report 83–28.* Sacramento: California State Postsecondary Education Commission, 1983b. (ED 234 857)

Gappa, J. M. "Employing Part-Time Faculty: Thoughtful Approaches to Continuing Problems," *American Association for Higher Education Bulletin,* 1984a, *(2),* 3–7.

Gappa, J. M. *Part-Time Faculty: Higher Education at a Crossroad.* ASHE-ERIC Higher Education Research Reports, no. 3. Washington, D.C.: Association for the Study of Higher Education, 1984b.

Kekke, R. "Who's Mr. Staff: Cheap Labor or Valued Resource?" Paper presented at the Central States Speech Association Conference, Lincoln, Nebr., April 7–9, 1983.

Leslie, D. W., Kellams, S. E., and Gunne, G. M. *Part-Time Faculty in American Higher Education.* New York: Praeger, 1982.

Melendez, W. A., and de Guzman, R. M. *Burnout: The New Academic Disease.* ASHE-ERIC Higher Education Research Reports, no. 9. Washington, D.C.: Association for the Study of Higher Education, 1983.

Quick, J. C., and Quick, J. D. *Organizational Stress and Preventive Management.* New York: McGraw-Hill, 1984.

Staples, K. "Money, Status, and Composition: Assumptions Underlying the Crisis of Part-Time Instruction." Paper presented at the College Composition and Communication Annual Meeting, New York, March 29–31, 1984. (ED 243 118)

Warshaw, L. J. *Managing Stress.* Reading, Mass.: Addison-Wesley, 1979.

Williams, J. E., and Johansen, E. "Career Disruption in Higher Education." *Journal of Higher Education,* 1985, *56* (2), 144–160.

Wilson, W. L. "The Use and Abuse of Part-Time Faculty: The Part-Timers' Point of View." Paper presented at the Speech Communication Association Convention, Chicago, November 2–4, 1984. (ED 252 119)

Judith M. Gappa is associate provost for faculty affairs at San Francisco State University. One of her responsibilities is the annual appointment of approximately one thousand part-time, temporary faculty members. She has previously held the positions of director of the Affirmative Action/Equal Opportunity Program at Utah State University and senior staff associate at the National Center for Higher Education Management Systems in Boulder, Colorado.

The problem of balancing personal and professional
aspirations is a principle source of stress in faculty lives,
but it has not been addressed by academia.

Faculty Stress: The Tension Between Career Demands and "Having It All"

Mary Deane Sorcinelli, Marshall W. Gregory

The tensions between personal life and professional work seem great for many academics, but have not received much discussion in academic literature. In a comment as notable for what it omits as for what it contains, Clara M. Lovett, dean of the College of Arts and Sciences at George Washington University, framed the professional issues this way (McMillen, 1986, p. 27): "We might, first of all, stop pretending that most of us can teach several courses, do significant work in the laboratory or library, and have enough energy left over to play significant roles in faculty governance." Clearly her reference to multiple professional roles raises important issues, but the comment makes no reference to the principal source of stress in faculty lives—the problem of adjusting professional work and personal living so that neither is slighted and both are fulfilled. She implies that problems of faculty stress are produced by the difficulty of balancing professional tasks. This view ignores the larger difficulty, immeasurably more complex, of balancing professional tasks—that are every bit as complicated as Lovett suggests—with the equally complex demands of private, family, and civic life.

    We would like to suggest a broader view of the problem. The set-

P. Seldin (ed.). *Coping with Faculty Stress.*
New Directions for Teaching and Learning, no. 29. San Francisco: Jossey-Bass, Spring 1987.

ting of our second morning of collaboration on this chapter illustrates the issue. Our work was set in the context of each of our spouses—full-time professionals themselves—having to take ill children to the doctor and pick up a car under repair, in order to give the two of us time as academics to concentrate on this chapter. This context of mingled professional and personal concerns is typical of many academics' lives, especially those with dual careers. It is not idiosyncratic to us. These are the issues that make up the texture of academics' everyday lives, yet comments on faculty stress frequently ignore this dimension of the problem. In our view, any formulation that fails to face the problems of balancing personal and professional aspirations will only be superficial.

In opening these issues for discussion, practically everything remains to be done. The topics are many and complicated and include the competing demands of careers, family aspirations, civic life, social relations, recreation, and ethical considerations. Our own extensive experience suggests that both the problems and the attendant emotions hit junior faculty members most strongly, and we shall rely heavily on our experience with these faculty members. Because they constitute the future of academic professionalism, their feelings and views on these matters are of long-range importance to academia. But this is merely a matter of emphasis. The truth is that these issues and problems cut across all ranks and disciplines and apply to both men and women.

The Push Toward Careerism

Academic careers are not merely work. Like other careers, they tend to become a way of life. The problem is that careers tend to become the whole life, and that a whole life defined this narrowly creates tensions. Professional work—career work—requires years of intensive training, and tends to demand a high and even absorbing level of commitment. It provides opportunities for lifelong professional growth but exhibits imperialistic tendencies. Career work not only spills over into personal life, but ultimately becomes the reference point in one's personal identity. When professionals are asked, "What do you do?" they almost always frame the answer in professional terms: "I'm a professor," "I'm an accountant," "I'm an attorney." Is it equally clear that campus nonprofessionals would so closely identify their sense of self with their jobs? If a nonprofessional's answer would place the work farther from the worker's identity—"I work over at the university"—what does the professional's likely collapse of the personal *into* the professional suggest about the nature of modern professionalism?

To make this distinction is not to patronize or generalize about the attitudes of nonprofessional workers. Our argument, rather, is that different occupations call for different levels and intensities of commitments, and that career occupations tend to become so compelling that the problem of how to live a life becomes overwhelmed by the question of how to make a career. As long as professionals are content to live this way, no problem exists. But many in academia would claim that they live under a different imperative: one of living the examined life, the complete life, the balanced life. To those dedicated to the life of the mind—a traditional formulation of the most fundamental academic value—the contradictions between the imperative of the whole and balanced life on the one hand, and the pressure to subsume all issues of living into career aspirations on the other, is a source of some guilt, much confusion, and great stress.

Too Many Roles, Too Few Models

Although one central source of stress on faculty members derives from the difficulty of making compatible the multiple roles and responsibilities they face at work and at home, another derives from the lack of role models. Feeling overloaded and fragmented seems endemic to an academic career. That academic life allows for a singular pursuit of knowledge with time for reflection is probably more illusion than reality. Faculty members are asked to do many different professional tasks—more than enough to fill one's entire life—and success is always measured against time. There is the unprecedented imperative to produce and to publish more, earlier, and faster. There is fierce competition to make a reputation ahead of one's peers, to become a "star" before the tenure clock stops ticking. There are teaching, advising, disciplinary, departmental, and campus activities, and the enticements and distractions of consulting.

And then there is time away from work. For many faculty members, work and life away from work form a seamless web—the results of reading, researching, and thinking in the library often appear clearly during the walk from office to home. While this overlap is rewarding, it is also potentially stressful. And increasingly, computers are bringing home and office closer together both physically and psychologically. Computer links make it even easier than in the past to continue working at home. Seamlessness between home and job may allow the job to become obtrusive and all-consuming. According to University of Iowa president James O. Freedman (1986, p. 92), "The absence of a clear boundary separating vocation from avocation, teaching from scholarship, creative effort from routine chores [permits] no single block of time . . . [to] be protected from a flood of conflicting but equally legitimate demands. . . . Because the search for knowledge is open-ended, there can be no point of conscientious rest."

The difficulty is intensified when career aspirations must be meshed with intimate relationships, care for children, and leisure and community activities. Working late into the evenings may mean not spending time with a spouse. Chairing a politically important committee meeting may mean not picking up a child from preschool. Volunteering in a community program may mean one less article on the *vita*. A young faculty member echoed this sentiment when he told us, "The toughest thing is to do a good job with a career that could consume all available time, pay attention to a spouse and children, publish or perish, teach well, lead an examined life, and keep out of debt."

The dilemma of too many roles is exacerbated by the problem of too few role models. Most faculty members, including today's junior faculty members, still have an ideal of the complete academician. This person, usually a man, had a helpmate to care for children and home, host the departmental colloquia, type the manuscripts, and organize family moves to the next, and better, university. Hochschild (1975, p. 67) argues that colleges and universities have shaped an almost singular model for success and, hence, a tacit policy toward the families of the faculty. If all else were equal, she asked, who would be most likely to survive under the career system—a man married to a full-time housewife and mother, or a man whose wife had a nine-to-five job and children in daycare, or a man who worked part-time, (as did his wife) while their children were small? She concludes, "To the extent that his family (1) does not positively help him in his work or (2) makes demands on his time and psychic energy that compete with those devoted to his job, they lower his chances for survival. This is true insofar as he is competing with other men whose wives either aid them or do not interfere with their work. Other things being equal, the university rewards the married family-free man."

The academic man has not been alone in his deferral of family commitments. The woman in academia was traditionally unmarried and childless. Almost all male faculty members marry at some point in their lives. But from one-third to one-half of female faculty members never marry or bear children. This statistic is even more telling when compared to the general population, in which 3 percent of adult women are single and 2 percent are childless (Freeman, 1977).

During the 1970s the traditional models enlarged to include the academic superwoman and, increasingly, the superman. While women struggled to climb the career ladder, many men were rethinking the role of "absentee father." Although it is true that academic women are only half as likely to be married as academic men, the proportion of married academic women has increased among the most recent female entrants (Finkelstein, 1984), intensifying conflicts between work and family roles. And many academic superwomen are learning that they have simply stepped into another trap. They commit themselves to overwhelming tasks and take on more work than they can perform creatively or healthfully. Many, in addition, feel compelled to crowd in career aspirations without letting anything else go. Upward-climbing academic men whose spouses are also on career tracks must now share the fatigue of coping with work, housekeeping, and childrearing. These men increasingly find themselves expected to fulfill traditional career goals and yet meet nontraditional family demands.

In the 1980s, both men and women are finding that the difficulties of building careers, cultivating personal relationships, and caring for children cannot be solved merely by throwing more energy into their tasks. They are beginning to see that the problem may not be their own failure to find solutions, but that, as academic professionalism has moved inexorably toward careerism, there may be no solutions that allow them to achieve both professional success and still preserve the traditional values and patterns of involvement in family and civic life.

Alternative Ways of Balancing It All

Faculty members choose different routes as they try to reconcile competing demands of work and personal life. Each has its benefits and costs. First, some faculty members still choose the traditional route in which the spouse operates as the domestic organizer, raising children, overseeing meals and housework, and investing her (still usually "her") identity in the professional spouse's work. This route is perhaps less frequently traveled by young faculty members—although it is certainly not rejected by all.

Second, other faculty members try to operate on a principle that one young woman described as "mini-maxi": In dual-career partnerships it is unlikely that both partners will find maximally satisfying and advantageous positions that allow them to live together; therefore, each agrees to settle for (at least) minimally acceptable working conditions if they can stay together. Going for the "mini" rather than the "maxi" allows the couple to define an acceptable life in which each has a voice.

Third, many faculty members make the unqualified decision simply to work overtime on the career, giving it precedence over family life, social or leisure time, and civic responsibilities. As one female assistant professor said, "I think the big turning point in deciding on an academic career was deciding whether I wanted to exclude as much of my life as my professors did for a career. And I realized that to be really good in my discipline, I would have to give up most of the rest of my life."

Ironically, sometimes poignantly, the gains in professional life become losses in personal life. Perhaps the stakes are highest for those who forgo marriage and children. The strains of commuter and two-career relationships lead some faculty members to feel that they can neither make nor sustain marriage and family commitments. Many junior faculty members whose tenure years run parallel to their biologically reproductive years avoid or defer having children. One woman who made such a choice and is now having trouble conceiving said to us, "If I can't have a child, I will always wonder if the costs of an academic career were too great."

Those who do bear children face the prospect, often troubling, of leaving them in the care of others for long periods during the day. Because no one, even family experts, yet knows the effects of extensive nonparental care on young children, such care becomes another source of acute guilt and family tension.

Personal Strategies

What strategies do faculty members employ for dealing with these problems? The question is especially important for junior faculty members, whose success or failure at developing strategies will determine the quality of their lives for the next twenty-five to thirty-five years. It is clear that no personal coping strategy—or set of strategies—will be adequate in themselves to solve the problems as they now exist. The problems are not grounded exclusively in individual vision, energy, dedication, or planning. These personal attributes make a difference but certainly not all the difference. The solutions require changes among the demands, attitudes, and values of disciplines and institutions as much as in personal strategies. But insofar as personal strategies may help at all, there are some that may make a difficult situation better, although none will make it go away.

Communication. In dual-career families, good communication is crucial to controlling stress. Faculty members today describe a constellation of issues they negotiate with spouses and children. Some recommend that couples consult on all career commitments, deciding how many times each will travel in a given month, when to decline or accept professional activities (perhaps disciplinary or university committees), how to deal with job offers, and how to keep spouses and children informed about demands of work to prevent unrealistic expectations. Individuals find it helpful to set rules for assignment of household tasks—who does the laundry, cooking, cleaning, shopping, and yardwork. Several feel it crucial to communicate expectations for children—whether to have any, when, how many, how much time to take off for childbirth, how to return to work, and so on.

Organization. Sometimes the stress of having too much to do at work and at home can be reduced by what one faculty member termed "thinking in advance." At work, some faculty members try to anticipate stressful periods (deadlines for articles or grades), plan ahead for such periods, and stagger them with a working spouse. Others draw up lists of what needs to be done and then figure out when they will be able to do each task. Another strategy is to plan a backup for emergencies or nonroutine situations such as sick children and car repairs. Some faculty members keep home responsibilities under control by listing tasks to be done around the house or using weekends to plan ahead for weekday meals, packing lunch boxes, and orchestrating the preschool carpool. A few people caution that organization can be overdone. One young faculty member described her life as so regimented that she found herself lying awake at night while the rest of the family slept, reviewing her laundry list of home and work tasks. Another person described cutting back on "dispensable" activities such as sleep, lunch, recreation, and talking with colleagues in the hall to have more time for work. But in general, faculty members working to strike a balance between total organization and chaos find that organizing eases the strains of managing scarce time and opposing demands.

Support. Faculty members need help from others, both in and beyond the family. In their personal relations, some faculty members make an effort to recognize and deal with signs of wear in their relationships. One faculty couple planned their teaching schedules so that they could schedule occasional lunches together, have the same evenings free, and have the same evenings booked for preparations and grading. Some simply find ways of asking each other for support, whether doing the dishes or taking on childcare during a stressful period such as tenure review.

Many faculty members look for support beyond the family. A few individuals try to recruit more help at work and delegate assignments to graduate assistants or secretaries. Some may desire to request reduced responsibilities from a department chair but few actually do. More often, faculty members reduce stress by "buying" their way out of dilemmas at home. Besides asking spouses and children for assistance, faculty members recommend hiring outside help. Many suggest having someone come to the home to tend a child, clean the house, or rake the lawn. For one faculty member, paying for help was tantamount to "buying sanity." But for a number of young faculty members supporting a family on one academic salary, such sanity may be prohibitively expensive. Finally, since many faculty members live far from immediate family and kin, they find it valuable to cultivate an extended family of university friends and neighborhood "grandparents" and rely on community agencies such as the YMCA and church daycare centers.

Flexibility. Remaining adaptable to change is significant in coping with work and family conflicts. Flexibility seems to operate on several levels, from taking turns bringing an ill child to a physician to taking turns advancing a career. Young faculty, particularly those with preschool children, are at a point at which their careers, like their small children, make inflexible demands on their time and energy. To bend with everyday hassles as well as occasional emergencies calls for cultivating not only coping strategies but a state of mind. Faculty members have described internal conversations in which they told themselves it would not be disastrous if they did not get all their work done, or if their child did not have quality attention at all times, or if the house was not immaculate, or if dinners were not elaborate. One concluded, "Put simply, people just have to decide what their priorities are."

Institutional Strategies

The connections among personal life, professional work, and institutional policies are unmistakable. The pressures of the academic workplace are too strong for faculty members to fight individually; institutions will have to encourage change. Sharing personal choices and strategies might help individual faculty members, but more benefits for more people will come from institutions rethinking their overall policies. Many faculty members seem to agree that institutions could assist them by being more flexible and supportive, especially in matters of recruitment and retention (relaxing tacit or formal policies on nepotism, institutional inbreeding, dual-career hiring, joint appointments, and time limits for tenure) and in providing more support for part-time work, parental leaves, and childcare.

It is industry, not academia, that is pointing to innovative policies and practices that can reduce the conflict between work and life away from work. An organization named Catalyst (1981) that works with corporations and individuals to develop career and family options reports that companies are not only identifying and analyzing career and family issues, but offering such solutions as on- or near-site childcare centers, childcare referral services, flexible benefits, flextime schedules, part-time work, job-sharing, work and family seminars, strategies for recruitment and retention of company couples, parental leaves, and special "personal days or credits" for meeting children's medical appointments or attending school conferences.

Although companies have no clear evidence, they now believe that accommodating the changing needs of families yields advantages in recruitment, retention, productivity, and morale. As an employer for General Mills Corporation (Gregg, 1986, p. 99) points out, "Any company that's going to go after the most productive and talented workforce is going to have to take into consideration a wide range of these issues." These are the very issues that colleges and universities will need to address if they hope to attract bright young people to the profession of teaching.

Final Concerns

As the academic ethos moves more and more toward a careerist model, certain broad questions emerge. What, for example, is the effect on persons, institutions, and ultimately, on society itself of the conflict between the fundamental academic value of living the examined, balanced life, on the one hand, and careerist pressures on the other? No one really knows. The question is seldom asked informally and even less frequently as the guiding question of research or serious inquiry.

Our own work in faculty development indicates that at both junior and senior levels many people feel frustrated and ambivalent about these conflicts. They have invested years and sometimes thousands of dollars in career training. They know they are skilled and are eager to show their expertise. They are vulnerable, then, to the suggestion that the exercise of their expertise is more important than anything else. Most academics, however, are personally reflective, and their long years of training in developed thought and research invite them to look at every issue from more than one perspective. Thus they are troubled by career demands that on the one hand seem so congenial and attractive but on the other seem oppressive and limiting.

At a personal level, what are the long-range implications of faculty continuing to "have it all," and implications for the way they work, for their health, and for their children and families? If, for example, academic couples continue to defer having children, or have fewer children than other segments of the population, can they count on future generations who will value and support education and intellectual commitment? If many women in academia continue to give up most of the rest of their lives for a career, can singular commitment to the life of the mind compensate for the lack of personal relationships, social life, marriage, and children? Will their model of academic life put off potential academics, especially young women who may see the career as too costly? What is the long-range, collective impact on marriage patterns (and the values that underlie marriage) of the dual-career and commuter marriages now so common in academia? Again, no one knows. But the questions offer fertile ground for inquiry.

At an institutional level, what are the effects on collegiality, work satisfaction, and, ultimately, life satisfaction of faculty members who believe that they have no time for anything but career tasks—and believe also that the narrowness of institutional policies and expectations only increases the stresses? Is collegiality, for example, undermined by competitiveness among faculty members who feel the pressure to publish earlier and more frequently than their colleagues? At some schools a work ethos emerges that pushes faculty members to spend weekends and evenings in the lab or office. What are institutional obligations for noticing these practices and creating an atmosphere in which standards for sane and productive scholarship can be developed apart from careerist pressures? What is the point of diminishing returns in expenditure of faculty energy? How much does the present frenetic pace of work cost persons and institutions in faculty burnout? At what level or point within institutions does one begin to ask the questions that will produce changes?

As for social implications, is a world characterized by narrow careerist ambitions the kind of world that most academic professionals really want to live in? After a few generations of professionals ignoring family and civic life, no matter how ruefully, can they count on preserving the kind of society they like best—a society of humane values and enlightened policies? If a humane and enlightened world is the kind of world most academics want to live in, what are their responsibilities for helping to create it? And does not the present difficulty that they experience in finding time and energy to think about these questions reflect a cluster of work values that contradict their other values?

It is impossible to be an academic today and not experience the pressure of these unanswered questions. It is also impossible to think that answers will emerge either easily or quickly. But if the discussion that will begin to produce answers, or at least creative strategies, is to begin, it must begin now.

References

Catalyst. *Corporations and Two-Career Families: Directions for the Future.* New York: Catalyst, 1981.

Finkelstein, M. J. *The Academic Profession.* Columbus: Ohio State University Press, 1984.

Freedman, J. O. "Point of View: The Professor's Life, Though Rarely Clear to Outsiders, Has Its Rewards—and Its Costs." *Chronicle of Higher Education,* February 19, 1986, p. 92.

Freeman, B. C. "Faculty Women in the American University: Up the Down Staircase." *Higher Education,* 1977, *6*, 165–170.

Gregg, G. "Putting Kids First." *New York Times Magazine,* April 13, 1986, p. 99.

Hochschild, A. R. " Inside the Clockwork of Male Careers." In F. Howe (ed.), *Women and the Power to Change.* New York: McGraw-Hill, 1975.

McMillen, L. "Job Competition, Unrealistic Expectations Said to Generate an Anxious Professoriate." *Chronicle of Higher Education,* March 26, 1986, p. 27.

Mary Deane Sorcinelli is director of faculty development and dean of the Faculties Office, Indiana University, Bloomington. She is the spouse of a faculty member and mother of three young children.

Marshall W. Gregory is an associate professor in the Department of English, Butler University, and director of the Postdoctoral Teaching Awards Program, Lilly Endowment, Inc. He is the spouse of a professional writer and father of two daughters.

This chapter describes several short-term self-help
techniques for coping with sources for faculty stress identified
in this sourcebook.

Short-Term Coping Techniques for Managing Stress

Anthony F. Grasha

Short-term coping techniques are relatively brief, focused, self-help interventions designed to help people manage stress more effectively. The coping strategies are oriented toward two stress-management goals: to (1) help reduce stress to more manageable levels and (2) prevent the recurrence of stressful events and stress-producing thoughts and behaviors. The suggestions presented in this chapter are based on effective short-term techniques for managing stress discussed in the stress-management literature (Adams, 1980; Brown, 1984), those techniques I have used consulting with faculty on teaching and other concerns (Fuhrmann and Grasha, 1983), and my experiences teaching self-help coping strategies and stress-management techniques in a variety of settings (Grasha, 1983; Grasha and Kirschenbaum, 1986). Each coping strategy is keyed to known causes of faculty stress emphasized in other chapters of this sourcebook.

Excessive Time Constraints

Life in an academic setting is often busy. The people who complain most about not having enough time to meet their commitments, however,

P. Seldin (ed.). *Coping with Faculty Stress.*
New Directions for Teaching and Learning, no. 29. San Francisco: Jossey-Bass, Spring 1987.

are often their own worst enemy. They usually agree to do too much and do not manage their time properly.

Be More Assertive. The inability to say "no" to the requests of students, administrators, and others is part of the problem. The willingness to say "no" is part of the solution. Unfortunately, too many people are afraid to say "no" because they fear negative consequences. It is not uncommon to hear faculty say such things as: "My students will be angry if I'm not available when they want," or "I can't refuse the dean's request; I'm up for promotion and my refusal will be held against me." Horrible consequences seldom occur after refusing a request. The real issue is the underlying fear of being disliked and rejected by others. People who truly like and admire us will remain friendly in spite of such refusals.

Saying "no" is a fundamental assertive skill that can help to prevent the overcommitment that leads to uncomfortable stress levels. The following suggestions are based on discussions found in Smith (1975) and Fensterheim (1975):

1. *Simply say "no" or "I don't want to do it."* There is no rule that requires a reason for refusing a request. In many cases, giving a reason only opens the door to counterarguments. It is sometimes best to look the other person in the eye, be firm, and stick with the decision.

2. *Repeat a message until the other party accepts it.* Sometimes those who request a favor do not listen carefully to the response. Thus it is often necessary to repeat a refusal before the message is understood.

3. *If someone asks for a reason, give one only if you feel that the other party obviously needs or could benefit from the information.* A department head or dean may benefit from knowing more about your work load. Thus your refusal does not appear arbitrary.

Set Priorities. People who complain of excessive time constraints are often guilty of doing more than they should under tight time schedules. It helps to gain a perspective on how time should be spent and what activities are more important than others. A quick way to accomplish the latter goal is to develop a list of activities for the week on Sunday evening. After listing the week's activities, answer the following questions about each item on the list:

1. Does the task have to be completed as scheduled?
2. Is the task something that can be delegated to others?
3. Can completion of the task be delayed for a period of time?
4. Is it really necessary to do this task at all?

Those activities that remain on the list can be scheduled at appropriate times during the week. When using this technique, two other issues must be considered. Sometimes demands for our time emerge during the week, and thus it is difficult to plan everything in advance. Therefore, use the questions to plan each day's activities and determine whether a request for your time should be accepted. Furthermore, when activities are eliminated from a schedule, avoid a natural tendency to completely fill the remaining time with other work-related tasks. Instead, schedule time to take breaks and to engage in enjoyable, relaxing, leisure-time activities. Taking a brisk walk or engaging in exercise are also good activities during such periods.

Relaxing leisure-time activities and physical activity are proven aids for reducing stress. They are more likely to be completed if placed on an appointment calendar. Just as we keep our appointments with others, we should nurture the habit of keeping appointments with ourselves.

Use Quick Relaxation Techniques. When daily activities become too stressful, muscular and mental tension increases. Taking a break to relax helps to decrease such tension. Relaxation devices also restore energy so that people can cope better with stressful events. The following methods can be used in a period of three to five minutes and are most beneficial when employed on a regular basis throughout the day.

Slow Rhythmic Breathing. Sit back in a chair or lie down if possible. Make your body as tense as you can and remain tense for a count of ten before releasing the tension. This will help to release muscle tension and facilitate relaxing. Now relax and inhale slowly through your nose for a count of four. Hold your breath for a count of four before exhaling slowly for a count of four. Once the slow breathing rhythm is established, some people find it helpful to repeat a pacifier word such as *calm, relax, peace,* or *quiet* to themselves while slowly breathing. Continue this slow breathing pattern for a period of three to five minutes.

Guided Imagery. While relaxed and using the slow breathing exercise, begin to imagine a pleasant scene in your mind. Mentally place yourself into the scene and enjoy the delights that you have imagined. You might, for example, imagine a series of scattered streams tumbling down a hillside. You follow the agitated energy of the water until it finally empties into a supremely quiet, tranquil pool or lake. The water has reached its level and now has no more need to rush and roar about. You remind yourself, while contemplating the tranquility of the deep pool, that all of us sometimes go along like the water passing through periods of seething stormy discontent. And then you see those periods of stormy discontent merging into the peacefulness of the undisturbed pool. Some people find that once such images are practiced and associated with relaxation, simply imagining the pleasant scene helps to calm them.

Writing to Relieve Tension. Writing can provide a release for inner tension. This was one of the functions faculty members reported that scholarly writing served in a study of faculty scholarship (Levi and Grasha, 1983). This effect has also been observed by people who keep a personal journal to record their observations about everyday frustrations, dilemmas, and problems (Progoff, 1975). It is also important to write about possible solutions. Finally, writing a letter that is not mailed, in which your frustrations with a person or event are described along with possible solutions, is helpful. Because writing can decrease tension, the process often leads to a clearer perspective on the nature of a problem and possible solutions to it.

Inadequate Resources

In addition to their normal work load, many faculty members find themselves having to type and collate exams, answer their phones, keep their files in order, maintain course records, run errands for class supplies, and make do with inadequate office space. Faculty members and administrators often differ about which of these services the institution should provide, and to what extent. As long as they fall below faculty expectations, such things can become irritations that may eventually increase stress levels (Brown, 1984). In addition, since many of these irritations are controlled by administrative budgets and priorities, faculty members often believe that they cannot control the problem and that the institution does not care about them. Feelings of alienation and dissatisfaction with the institutions develop and in turn add to job stress.

Although institutional budgets are largely responsible for inadequate resources, this does not mean that teachers are helpless to change some things. Unfortunately, the problem is usually defined in terms of "How can my college do a better job of getting me resources to do my job?" When the problem is reframed and restated as, "What can I do to help myself get needed resources?" other possible solutions emerge.

In response to inadequate secretarial resources, faculty members are utilizing computers in greater numbers, often with institutional assistance for their purchase. The computer significantly assists in processing course records and handouts, writing scholarly material, and preparing exams. Computerized test banks can organize an exam and cut a stencil in less than thirty minutes. When stored on computer, course syllabi and handouts also can be modified quickly and reissued. Electronic devices, in general, are now inexpensive enough so that faculty members can use them to reduce many of the minor stresses of working within bureaucratic frameworks.

High Self-Expectations and Personal Insecurity

William James (1892), describes a commonly accepted relationship between expectations and self-esteem. Expectations lead to insecurity when a person's achievements fall short of what is expected (see Chapter Two). This may occur when a deficiency in meeting goals occurs or when someone possesses unrealistic expectations. Under ideal conditions, self-esteem would increase when the number of achievements exceeds an individual's expectations.

Unfortunately, a characteristic of many upwardly mobile people is that they tend to discount their achievements and thus feel insecure about their accomplishments. In spite of significant achievements, Levi and Grasha (1983) found that highly productive faculty members believed they had not accomplished enough. However, even those persons who were relatively less productive as scholars felt unhappy and insecure. They worried that they had not accomplished as much as was expected of them by others. In both groups, their achievements failed to match their expectations.

Readjust Expectations. Decreasing the number of personal expectations or goals can help to improve self-esteem provided what is achieved continues to exceed those lowered expectations. There are three ways to achieve this. First, faculty members should administer friendly and frequent reminders to themselves of how high self-expectations may adversely affect self-esteem. This can serve as a catalyst to modify those expectations. Second, they should expand the time frame for meeting expectations. Ambitious people want the trappings of success in a short amount of time. A friend expected within eighteen months to complete two books, write three major grant proposals, serve on several government research review boards, teach and conduct research, and serve as an acting department head. He failed to accomplish everything he wanted and was unhappy. Had he set a three- or four-year time frame, he would have been more successful. Third, it is important to consider whose expectations one is trying to achieve. It is not unusual for faculty members to want certain things because department heads, deans, colleagues, and mentors have convinced them that they need them. Thus, they pursue what others want for them and not necessarily what they desire for themselves. By concentrating on pursuing personally relevant goals, the number of expectations decreases.

One way to accomplish this goal is to develop a list of goals one would like to accomplish as a faculty member. Each item on that list should be analyzed carefully to determine whether it is something "I really want," or if it is a goal that "others think I need, but I am not convinced that I really do." Personal priorities for spending time should be oriented toward the former and not the latter.

Seek Small Wins. While expectations can be readjusted, it is also helpful to maximize the chances of achieving those goals. People feel better about themselves when they complete what they set out to accomplish and do so in a satisfactory manner. One strategy is to seek small wins. That is, establish overall goals and then focus on the smaller objectives needed to accomplish the larger goal. In effect, this gives us "mini-achievements" and benchmarks to assess progress. Small successes breed motivation and confidence to continue working on much larger tasks. They also help manage stress by making what might be perceived as unmanageable much more manageable.

A client wanted to redesign her introductory biology course. She chose the summer before classes began to attempt a major overhaul of the course. Her plan was ambitious and included designing self-study modules for students, acquiring the latest audiovisual materials, designing new lectures and overhead transparencies, and gathering thirty-five-millimeter slides of important material. She quickly became overwhelmed. At my suggestion, she began to think of the course redesign as a two-year process in which she could accomplish much smaller objectives during each academic quarter. Thus she spent the summer redesigning her lectures and gathering information on audiovisual materials. The other tasks were completed on schedule later.

Focus on Achievements. When the number of expectations exceeds the number of achievements, it is easy to focus only on what has not been accomplished instead of celebrating what has been accomplished. The reason is that anxiety is aroused when incompleted tasks await completion. While this anxiety may provide energy to complete such tasks, it can also interfere with appreciating what has been completed. Periodic and frequent reminders of accomplishments are needed to boost self-confidence.

Use Coping Self-Statements. When under stress, what one says to oneself adds to the problem. It is common to find people making statements that hold them back or contribute to mistakes. To counter such thinking, Meichenbaum (1977) reports that positive self-statements can help reduce stress associated with achieving goals. These include frequent reminders such as "You can do it, you have done similar things before," "Take it easy and do it as you planned," and "That was well done." Meichenbaum finds that coping self-statements work best when people frequently remind themselves of past successes, give themselves appropriate directions for current tasks, administer private pep talks when needed, and reward themselves for successfully completing a task.

Seek Social Support. Social support can serve as a protective buffer to diminish the effects of stress (LaRocco and others, 1980; see also Chapter Five). The comfort of other people provides a sympathetic ear, encouragement, advice, and a chance to interact with people who have confidence in one's ability to succeed. As a result, social support is a powerful intervention for managing stress and has been shown to enhance the self-confidence and problem-solving abilities of persons experiencing unacceptable levels of tension.

Peer development groups have been successfully employed to help faculty members cope with problems in their teaching (Sweeney and Grasha, 1979). The process involves three colleagues, within or across disciplines, agreeing to consult with each other on the issues they face in the classroom. They discuss their goals for a course and the difficulties they experience achieving those goals. They make observations of class sessions and discuss what they observed. There is no reason a similar arrangement

could not be employed to discuss other job-related issues. Shor
arrangement, agreements to have lunch, a drink after work, or
meeting to discuss common problems can also help.

To use support groups demands that one take the initiative to con-
vene such a group. To do this, however, an attitude barrier must be overcome. This is the perception of faculty members I have interviewed that "I
can do what needs to be done by myself." This independence may only
continue to isolate people who could benefit from the support of others.

Influence over Departmental Affairs

The perception that one cannot influence departmental or college
affairs can be stressful. While influencing departmental affairs is a complex issue, there are two components that lend themselves to short-term
strategies. First, take steps to ensure that various requests are heard. Second, find out whether one has as little control as one believes.

Make Requests Assertively. A key element in influencing others is
to state what is desired in a manner that is clear, concise, and that increases
the chances of obtaining the desired outcome. A process for making such
requests called a *DESC script* (Bower and Bower, 1976) is often useful.
The elements of a DESC script are outlined below.

1. **D**escribe the situation to another person: State how you see it
and focus on behaviors you have observed that will form the background
for your request.

2. **E**xpress how you feel about the situation: Relate the positive
and negative feelings and reservations you have about the circumstances
that concern you.

3. **S**pecify what you want: Make a clear, concise statement of what
you want to have happen in terms of specific behaviors you would like to
observe.

4. **C**onsequences: Indicate likely consequences if your request or
proposal is carried out and possible negative consequences if it is not. As
a general rule, focus on the positive benefits.

A DESC script can be written out in advance and practiced before
it is used. Although it helps to organize a request, and it helps people to
follow an argument, it is no guarantee of success. Alternative and other
compelling points of view are possible. Thus one must be prepared to
compromise and accommodate other points of view. People who are unwil-
ling to do the latter are often those who experience the largest amounts of
stress trying to influence others.

Develop a Personal Plan for Change. People may forget how much
influence they have had. Gaining a realistic perspective on this issue may
reduce stress levels as well as suggest ideas for how to influence events. To
gain perspective, fold a sheet of paper in half. Across the top of the left-

hand side write, "Departmental issues that I have helped to influence." Across the right-hand half write, "Departmental issues that I have not been able thus far to influence." The former reminds one that some successes of influence have occurred. The latter acknowledges that influence takes time.

From the right-hand side of the list, prioritize issues that are personally important. The issue selected for further work should meet the following criteria: (1) It is important enough to spend some time on; (2) it does not represent an overly difficult task; and (3) at least one or two other people would be interested in developing a plan for change. After completing this assessment, a plan of action is developed. The plan should be developed with other people who share the same concern. Collective attempts of change generally work better than those initiated by persons who are overly frustrated by their past failures. Having colleagues involved in the same efforts also provides needed social support for the effort. Such support can make the process of change less frustrating than it would otherwise become.

Interactions with Students

The demands of planning and meeting classes, grading and advising students, judging appeals over grades, and coping with conflicts in class over ideas and personalities create more than their share of unwanted anxiety, frustration, and tension.

Develop Clear Evaluation Procedures. In Chapter Two, Peter Seldin indicates that concerns over evaluating students are a cause of stress in teachers' relationships with students. Although there is no ideal way to assess student performance, Carter (1977) reports that such concerns generally decrease when grading policies meet the following criteria.

Objectivity. The criteria on which grades are based should be explicitly stated during the first class session. In particular, how a given course grade relates to such matters as exam points students must earn, the quality expected of assignments, and any extra credit options should be specified in advance.

Accuracy. Instructors should have specific and unambiguous data on students. Thus objective tests and essay tests in which clearly defined answers are specified will be more accurate than those exams that place a heavy reliance on subjective impressions of the instructor.

Mastery of Content. Students should be informed of the content objectives of the course and the degree to which they are expected to master them. Exams should be based on those content objectives.

Flexibility. The composition of student ability in a class varies somewhat from term to term, and one's exams are not always equally difficult. A grading system should be flexible in the face of such variations. Thus it is important not to adhere to ideas that there should be a certain number of high- or low-letter grades or that only a small number of students should receive high grades.

Consider Student Learning Styles. Student learning styles can be described as competitive, collaborative, independent, dependent, avoidant, and participant (Fuhrmann and Grasha, 1983). Each style contributes to the learning style profile for a given student and the entire class. A source of discomfort for teachers occurs when the teaching methods favor one or two styles and ignore the others. Thus a traditional lecture method may encourage the more dependent and competitive students and leave those who prefer collaborative and independent learning experiences somewhat frustrated. However, teaching methods may lead to low levels of participation and a tendency for students to avoid attending class. The dissatisfaction students experience leaves many instructors frustrated. "I try my best and some students just don't appreciate what I do" is a common complaint.

The appropriate use of learning styles helps to increase instructor and student satisfaction with a course (Fuhrmann and Grasha, 1983). Using a variety of teaching methods can help accomplish this objective. Furthermore, establishing classroom goals and then determining how each goal could be achieved by encouraging particular learning styles can help. In particular, teaching in collaborative, independent, and dependent styles allows for variety in the classroom. Thus, if students are expected to become familiar with the three facets of Sigmund Freud's personality theory, the instructor might do the following according to the respective learning styles:

1. Give independent students a study guide of Freud's theory and then let them search for books in the library to answer each question.
2. Place collaborative students into small groups of three and give each an aspect of Freud's theory to research. During class, students meeting in small groups could teach each other about what they have discovered. The instructor would be available to answer questions and solicit opinions from each group as a culminating activity.
3. Give dependent students a lecture on Freud and have students take notes.

The intent is not to have three ways of teaching every classroom goal. Instead, the process is designed to introduce variety into a course to prevent the tension some faculty members experience from a lack of such variety. The instructor can introduce such options immediately and does not have to wait until the beginning of a term.

Dispute Irrational Beliefs. How people think about events in their life affects how they feel (Ellis, 1973). One of the important classes of beliefs that affect our emotions and subsequent interactions are what Ellis terms *irrational*. Thoughts and verbal statements that present thoughts in extreme and absolute ways, are clues to their presence. Extreme words include, among others, *all, every, always, awful, terrible, horrible, totally,* and *essential*. Absolute words suggest an absence of choices and include the terms *must, should, have to, need,* and *ought*. When such language is combined with thoughts that do not fit the objective facts of a situation, lead to negative emotions, interfere with our interactions with others, and prevent us from making plans for the future, irrational beliefs have taken hold. Their presence is seen in the following statements from clients with whom I have worked: "Oh, that idea for running a class will never work. I once tried discussion groups and they failed." "I knocked my brains out working for this department and no one really cares about my efforts." "I'll never be any good running this committee. Some people have what it takes and others like me do not."

When caught in the stress produced by irrational beliefs, it is important to dispute them. A dispute may occur in two ways: One is to challenge the validity of the beliefs that affect the emotion. For example, "Just because discussion groups didn't work once is hardly a good reason to assume they will never work. I probably need to do some things differently." "It is really unfair to say that no one cares about what I do. I have received positive comments from people in the department for my efforts. I am overreacting to what one person said at the last meeting." "How can I be sure that I will never be any good running a committee? Surely there are some skills involved that I currently do not have that I can learn." Having challenged their validity, the second step in disputing them is to take actions that support the challenge. In the respective examples above, each person was encouraged to experiment with discussion group techniques, talk with others in the department to determine their perceptions of him or her, and practice using several techniques for running a meeting.

To be successful, the short-term strategies outlined in this chapter must be integrated into a person's professional and often personal conduct. Such an integration is unlikely to occur unless one accepts the challenge of managing stress, becomes committed to using a coping strategy, practices using it, and monitors its effectiveness with the intention of making necessary corrections.

References

Adams, J. D. *Understanding and Managing Stress: A Workbook in Changing Lifestyles.* San Diego, Calif.: University Associates, 1980.

Bower, S. A., and Bower, G. A. *Asserting Yourself: A Practical Guide for Positive Change.* Reading, Mass.: Addison-Wesley, 1976.

Brown, B. B. *Between Health and Illness.* Boston: Houghton Mifflin, 1984.

Carter, K. R. "Student Criteria Grading: An Attempt to Reduce Some Common Grading Problems." *Teaching of Psychology,* 1977, *4,* 59–62.

Ellis, A. *Humanistic Psychotherapy: The Rational Emotive Approach.* New York: Julian Press, 1973.

Fensterheim, H. *Don't Say Yes When You Want to Say No.* New York: McKay, 1975.

Fuhrmann, B., and Grasha, A. F. *A Practical Handbook for College Teachers.* Boston: Little, Brown, 1983.

Grasha, A. F. *Practical Applications of Psychology.* Boston: Little, Brown, 1983.

Grasha, A. F., and Kirschenbaum, D. S. *Adjustment and Competence: Concepts and Applications.* St. Paul, Minn.: West, 1986.

James, W. *The Principles of Psychology.* Vol. 1. New York: Henry Holt, 1892.

LaRocco, J. M., House, J. S., and French, J. R. "Social Support, Occupational Stress, and Health." *Journal of Health and Social Behavior,* 1980, *21,* 202–218.

Levi, L., and Grasha, A. F. "Motivational Processes and Personal Attributes of Writers." Paper presented at American Psychological Association meetings, Anaheim, Calif.: August 26, 1983.

Meichenbaum, D. *Cognitive-Behavior Modification.* New York: Plenum, 1977.

Progoff, I. *At a Journal Workshop.* New York: Dialogue House Library, 1975.

Smith, M. J. *When I Say No, I Feel Guilty.* New York: Dial Press, 1975.

Sweeney, J. M., and Grasha, A. F. "Improving Teaching Through Faculty Development Triads." *Educational Technology,* 1979, *19,* 54–57.

Anthony F. Grasha is a professor in the Department of Psychology, College of Arts and Sciences, at the University of Cincinnati. He is the former director of the University of Cincinnati's Faculty Resource Center and Institute for Research and Training in Higher Education.

Techniques are available that enable us to decrease stress to more reasonable and productive levels.

Long-Term Stress Management

James L. Noel

Academics are often thought of as living in an "ivory tower" world, somehow immune to the tensions and pressures of everyday life. But in reality, academics, like other people, must cope with the stresses inherent in living in the late twentieth century. They work in large, complex organizations, have time demands and deadlines, interact with a diversity of people in the course of the day, and have families and mortgages. And like their peers in business, industry, and the professions, academics must learn to manage their stress.

Mallinger (1986) proposes that stress management is an organizational as well as an individual responsibility. Organizations can reduce stress by taking preventive measures. Job redesign, decentralization of authority, innovative reward systems, improvements in communications networks, refining performance evaluation standards, and clarifying role expectations may be required to lower employee uncertainty and feelings of helplessness on the job (see Chapter Eight).

The tenure process is a source of stress for many academics. To apply Mallinger's thesis, institutions can reduce the stress associated with tenure by clarifying the performance standards by which tenure decisions are made. This would reduce the ambiguity of the tenure process. Tenure decisions based on explicit and understandable criteria are far more likely to be perceived as fair.

Although academic institutions have an obligation to moderate

P. Seldin (ed.). *Coping with Faculty Stress.*
New Directions for Teaching and Learning, no. 29. San Francisco: Jossey-Bass, Spring 1987.

organizational stress, it is unrealistic to expect them to be transformed into ideal settings. Improvements in individual stress-management strategies are also necessary. The focus of this chapter is on those long-term strategies that academics can use to decrease the detrimental impact of stress on their lives.

Stress is a Personal Experience

Stress is a condition that takes place within one's own body and is a highly individual, subjective state. Each individual's specific response to stress is unique due to factors such as genetic potential, general state of health and fitness, and previous experience in dealing with stress. Everyone experiences some degree of stress virtually all the time. Some academics do their best work under stress. In this sense, stress has a positive impact. Problems relating to stress are apparent when there is too much stress, or too much for too long. The intensity and duration of stress one can endure depend on individual capacity.

One cannot eliminate stress, but one can attempt to manage the stress in his or her life. Stress can lead to either disease or increased energy and achievement. Its impact will depend on how the stressed person responds. Selye (1975), one of the pioneers of stress theory, calls stress that is challenging and satisfying *eustress*, meaning "good" stress. He refers to stress that is damaging as *distress*.

Stressors and the Manifestation of Stress

Stressors are the internal or external factors that trigger a stress reaction in a person. Time pressures associated with the end of a semester are examples of external stressors. The internal expectation of being promoted to full professorship is an internal stressor. Whether internal or external, stressors place a demand on the person and the result is the stress he or she experiences.

It has been documented that much of the marked increase in stress-related disorders can be related to an accelerated pace of living. The well-known study of Holmes and Rahe (1967) resulted in the Social Readjustment Rating Scale, an index of common life change events. Numerical values were assigned to forty-three typical events such as changing jobs, marrying, giving birth to a child, or relocating; positive as well as negative events were included. The authors' systematized method of correlating life events with the onset of illness demonstrates that neurophysiological imbalance can be precipitated by normal life events that are perceived as stressful. Such an imbalance may lead to the onset of psychological or physical stress-related disorders.

Learning to live with stress requires a recognition of one's own manifestation of stress. This is not easy for many because the manifestations of stress cover a wide range of behaviors that are both physical and emotional in nature. Symptoms of prolonged stress include: overeating or lack of appetite, excessive smoking or drinking, irritability, insomnia, chronic fatigue or depression, numerous physical complaints or disorders, emotional outbursts, and unexplained lapses in performance and memory. This list of manifestations of stress can certainly be expanded. Each person may identify behavior in the list that he or she has exhibited during stressful periods. Managing stress requires that people identify these and similar behaviors and know when they have violated their personal tolerance for stress.

Managing Stress

The methods presented here for managing stress are based on long-term changes in life-style. Most of the methods will not be new to academics, who are far more health-conscious today than they were only twenty years ago. Because stress is a highly individualized process, each person must develop his or her personalized program for managing stress. The techniques presented cover a range of alternatives that research has shown to be effective. No one technique is a universal solution for stress relief. Stress is too complex and individualized for a single approach. Each technique will have value for some academics but not for all. Success lies in identifying those techniques that are most effective for each person as he or she learns to manage stress.

Chemical Stressors

Tobacco, alcohol, caffeine, tranquilizers, and other drugs are recognized potential stressors. Prolonged or excessive use can be harmful. It is paradoxical that for many the most common methods of seeking immediate stress reduction are themselves stressors. The coffee and cigarette break or the extra drink before dinner, for example, are often used to "promote relaxation."

Drugs and medication are foreign substances that must be considered potential stressors even when taken to relieve the symptoms of stress. There are stress-related situations in which the ease of medication is justified, particularly on a short-term basis. However, extreme dependence on external substances such as drugs can mask stress and give the illusion of well-being so that basic problems are not confronted. Those seeking a life-style change compatible with managing the stress in their lives should stop smoking and moderate their consumption of caffeine and alcohol. There are workshops, courses, and organizations solely dedicated to helping those who have become dependent on one or more of these substances.

The major requirement is a commitment to give up the dependency. Denial of potential harm is the primary obstacle.

Nutrition

There is an intricate set of interactions between nutrition and stress. In some of his earlier studies, Selye (1970) found that "stress, perhaps the most nonspecific reaction form of living organisms, can be both the cause and consequence of malnutrition" (p. 2).

Proper nutrition can be decisive in bolstering the body's resources. A diet that is deficient in any of the major food groups or minerals or vitamins, and is sustained over time, will contribute to stress symptoms. For many, this means revising the typical American diet to include more whole, fresh, natural foods and decreasing amounts of prepared or processed foods. This would reduce some of the nutritional problems resulting from excessive amounts of refined carbohydrates, salts, fats, and oils in the diet. The increased intake of excessive amounts of animal protein combined with the reduced intake of proteins from natural grains or natural fiber foods has been linked to the growing incidence of bowel cancer and chronic intestinal diseases.

Excessive food can also be considered a stressor because any substance that is not used nutritionally by the body becomes yet another toxin or foreign substance to be processed or eliminated. Obesity and its long-term effects on health, especially heart disease, has been well documented and can be considered a national health problem. Paradoxically, overeating is often a manifestation of the individual's attempts to deal with stress.

Physical Ability

Physical activities performed regularly aid in stress reduction. Regular exercise develops new and greater capacities in several areas of body functioning, especially when the exercises push the system to approximately twice the resting heart rate for briefly sustained periods. Strength and stamina are increased, which contributes to a level of health that can withstand the stress of modern living.

The major emphasis now in physical activity programs is aerobic exercise. Proponents of aerobic exercise claim that it strengthens the heart, lungs, and muscles throughout the body and improves circulation. Studies indicate that regular, sustained activity such as that used in aerobic exercise reduces blood pressure and decreases heart rate. Rigorous sustained activities that increase the demand on the heart and promote more efficient functioning of the body include bicycling, running or jogging, skiing, swimming, vigorous skating, and jumping rope. Other activities, such as a brisk uninterrupted walk or a regular game of tennis, although not considered aerobic exercise, can equally benefit the more sedentary person who is not in condition for more rigorous activity.

The success of any regular, sustained activity program depends on selecting an activity that is truly enjoyable and can be adopted as part of a life-style change. If the labor itself adds to or causes frustration, it provides no benefits. Further, it is wise to consult a physician before beginning an exercise program. A physical exercise program conducted with proper guidance does not push the system too far or too fast. The exercise should to be regular and sustained, enjoyable, and easily incorporated into one's life-style. A hobby or avocation that allows for creativity and fun is another major stress-reduction outlet. No matter what the activity, it should be given full attention if only for a few minutes a day. Again, the activity should provide enjoyment.

Relaxation Techniques

There are a variety of ways to relax and slow the physical and mental processes. Activities such as transcendental meditation, bioenergetics, autogenics, and biofeedback, can be used regularly to provide a time during the day to relax and experience more energy within one's self.

Some relaxation techniques can be learned relatively quickly. Benson (1975) identifies the basic elements of meditation. He disassociates it from cult or religious overtones and calls it the "relaxation response." His technique is simple and can be used as an introduction to the practice of meditation. The elements of Benson's technique are found in many other relaxation methods. During the relaxation response, the person sits quietly with eyes closed, repeating a single sound such as the word "one" while disregarding extraneous thoughts. By fixing attention on a single task for a protracted period of time, the meditator is able to overcome the mind's habit of moving rapidly from one thought to another. Focusing attention on a single object or word is necessary to quiet the mind and allow images to form without distraction. With continued practice and experimentation, people can gradually increase their ability to regulate attention and reduce the mind's tendency to generate incessant activity and distractions.

There are other techniques short of formal meditation that academics may want to use. A change of pace or scenery can bring about immediate stress relief. People can take a brief walk across campus, listen to music for a few minutes, massage the face and forearms briefly, or look out a window at a tree or people walking across campus. These are all examples of brief interruptions that can help reduce momentary stress if they are done with intent and attention.

Coping with Disappointment

A popular female vocalist asks the question, "Is that all there is?" Disappointments and unmet expectations are common in life. Inability to cope with these feelings is a source of stress in one's life. All people have goals or dreams toward which they aspire. For some, it may be the desire to be department head or dean; for others, it might be writing the definitive work in their area, or research that provides a major breakthrough. Some will achieve their objectives. Many will labor in relative obscurity, competent at what they do but not likely to earn a Nobel prize.

Stress is a personal experience, and stress exists in perceptions of events, not in events themselves. Stress is internal and is based on people's expectations. If one is fortunate, one overcomes disappointments quickly. If one is not fortunate, one may dwell on disappointments and become miserable, tense, or depressed, which adds to the stress level. Unmet expectations create a sense of loss—not of an object or person, but an idea. Enthusiasm and direction may also be lost. Stress responses may reflect dissatisfaction with self; a negative self-image; or a sense of alienation, hopelessness, and powerlessness.

Coping with stress generated by disappointment and unmet expectations requires that one develop a sense of realism about his or her expectations. These suggestions may be of value:

1. Know your abilities and expectations. Do not set expectations beyond reach or reality.

2. Eliminate absolute and exacting expectations. No single anticipated outcome is essential.

3. Maintain a flexible attitude. Be ready to revise expectations.

4. Be willing to accept disappointment.

5. When disappointed, accept the associated emotions—hurt, anger, or sadness. Do not claim not to be disappointed. Express feelings and move beyond them to gain perspective on the loss.

6. Learn from past disappointments. Every letdown is a lesson in reality, giving the opportunity to readjust expectations or design a new plan of action to meet the original expectation.

Emotional Support

We all need someone with whom we can talk and share our private feelings—our hurts and our triumphs. Within our families or among friends, we need to build a network that can provide us with positive attention, recognition, and appreciation on a consistent basis. We all need to be appreciated and acknowledged for our own uniqueness and worth.

A good listener is always a source of help in times of stress. Straight, sympathetic, understanding listening can help relieve stress. We feel unburdened, and less alone; there is less of a feeling of being wrong, bad, or angry. Sometimes, too, we gain clarity because we decrease our stress and can think clearly again.

In terms of stress arising from the academic environment, it often helps to have a peer with whom one can share feelings (see Chapter Six). A person who experiences stress may be relieved by talking to someone who is also experiencing the same type of stress. Peers, especially, can appreciate one's stress because they, too, are experiencing it. Building a network of peer relationships takes time, effort, and reciprocity. It will, however, serve as a powerful mechanism for stress relief. To assess peers and others who may help alleviate stress, consider the following qualities. A good listener is someone who (1) is not judgmental, (2) shows interest, (3) keeps confidences, (4) understands and cares, and (5) has feelings of empathy and compassion.

I have observed that academics may have a tendency to be one-dimensional. They invest heavily in satisfaction associated with the academic environment without diversifying their emotional involvement. However, involvement in the community and developing friendships outside of academic circles is helpful. If the academic environment becomes stressful, one who has diversified his or her emotions into a number of other activities is more able to cope with stress.

Assertiveness and Time Management

Two skills closely associated with successful stress management are assertiveness and time management. Consider the following scenario:

Dr. Paula Brown, chair of the English Department, enters the office of Assistant Professor Robert Jones. "Bob," Dr. Brown asks, "Do you have your spring course outlines? They were due last week." Flustered, Bob replies, "It can't be that time already!" With a hint of a friendly smile Dr. Brown responds, "Funny how time flies when you're having fun." Turning to leave Bob's office, Dr. Brown stops and turns toward Bob again. "By the way, Bob," she asks, "have you turned in copies of your final exams? I don't remember seeing them." "Paula," Bob responds, "I am way behind schedule. I guess I got sidetracked when Bill asked me to help him put together some materials for the curriculum committee on the course we're going to team-teach." "But Bob, that material isn't needed by the curriculum committee until March," Dr. Brown says in surprise. "I know," Bob responds, "but Bill was so anxious to get started, I just wanted to please him. He was so insistent." "Paula," Bob exclaims, "it just seems that I've lost control over time, and the harder I work, the less I get done!"

In this scenario, Bob is having difficulty managing his time, which is probably compounded by his lack of assertiveness, as shown in his relationship with Bill. It is beyond the limits of this short chapter to discuss

72

time management or assertiveness in any great detail. Considerable literature on both of these skills is readily available as are seminars and short
courses often offered by universities. However, there is value in briefly
reviewing the relationship between stress management and time management and assertiveness.

Like Bob, academics seem to continually encounter stressful situations because they never have enough time. The lack of proper time management results in a decreased level of job satisfaction, which in turn adds
to the internal stress level. With improved time management, one can
increase his or her performance levels, thereby increasing work satisfaction
and decreasing stress. In addition, a lack of assertiveness frequently causes
problems. Like Bob, academics may take on projects because they do not
want to displease colleagues. The result may be having so much to do
that one can do nothing well.

Learning to assert oneself gains one respect and decreases reactions
to stress. Assertive behavior makes it possible for academics, to act in their
best interest without undue anxiety and to express their feelings comfort-
ably. Assertiveness is exercising one's rights without denying the rights of
others.

Conclusion

Stress is an inherent part of life, and academics, like others, need to
learn to manage their stress. A wide range of techniques that will enable
academics to decrease their stress to more reasonable and productive levels
have been presented. Those seeking to manage their stress should develop
a personalized program for life-style change and work hard to maintain
this change over the long run.

Throughout this chapter I have discussed stress as a personal experience. Each of us must find our own innate stress level and live accordingly. Reducing the stress in our lives means clarifying our values,
separating the significant from the insignificant, and understanding what
we can control. The secret, as Selye (1975) points out, is not to live less
intensely, but more intelligently.

References

Benson, H. *The Relaxation Response.* New York: William Morrow, 1975.
Holmes, H., and Rahe, R. "The Social Readjustment Rating Scale." *Journal of Psychosomatic Research*, 1967, *2* (4), 213-218.
Mallinger, M. "Stress Management: An Organizational and Individual Responsi-bility." *Training and Development Journal*, 1986, *40* (2), 16-17.
Selye, H. "On Just Being Sick." *Nutrition Today*, 1970, *4* (2), 2-10.
Selye, H. *Stress Without Distress.* Philadelphia: Lippincott/Signet, 1975.

James L. Noel is program manager of business management courses, Executive Education, General Electric Company. Before joining the General Electric Company, he was dean of continuing education at Auburn University in Montgomery, Alabama.

Stress is an inevitable characteristic of academic life, yet effective institutional preventive stress management can avert distress.

Institutional Preventive Stress Management

James C. Quick

Stress is an inevitable characteristic of academic life (see Chapters Two, Three, and Four). However, it is not inevitable that academic *stress* become *distress*. Preventive stress management offers the hope that, in formulating individual and institutional responses to stress, the health and well-being of employees will be enhanced by averting the distressful consequences of stressful events.

Preventive stress management has been defined as "an organizational philosophy and set of principles which employs specific methods for promoting individual and organizational health while preventing individual and organizational distress" (Quick and Quick, 1984a, p. 146). Within this framework, the current focus is on institutional rather than individual action. Preventive stress management is founded on five underlying principles: (1) individual and organizational health are interdependent, (2) management has a responsibility for individual and organizational health, (3) institutional and organizational distress are not inevitable, (4) each individual and organization reacts uniquely to stress, and (5) organizations are dynamic and ever-changing entities (Quick and Quick, 1984a). The third principle is central: It embodies the hope of preventive stress management. The other principles are directly relevant to institutional preventive stress management in two ways.

P. Seldin (ed.). *Coping with Faculty Stress.*
New Directions for Teaching and Learning, no. 29. San Francisco: Jossey-Bass, Spring 1987.

First, if administrators in academic institutions are going to act on the second principle and fulfill their responsibilities, then they must appreciate the fourth principle. There are no two institutions or two individuals with the same history or current conditions. This fact requires administrators to have a specific grasp of both their institution's and their faculty's unique characteristics. Failure to develop this understanding may lead to the ineffective application of the preventive actions discussed. In a sense, the application of institutional preventive stress management is as much an art form as a science.

Second, the notion of individual-institutional interdependence, as reflected in the first principle, suggests that preventive actions by both parties are appropriate. The focus here will not, however, be on individual change strategies such as exercise. Institutionalizing these individual change strategies through fitness clubs or programs in the university does not constitute institutional action. Rather, the institution itself must engage in planned action under the rubric of the fifth principle. This means that the institution will change over time so as to minimize or eliminate unnecessary and unreasonable demands not essential to an institution's functioning. At the same time, the institution should progress toward providing resources to faculty and staff to manage the necessary and reasonable demands of academic life.

The Nature of Academia: Program Design Considerations

There are at least three considerations that should be addressed in the development of a specific prevention program. These are the freedom of academia, the complexity of academic institutions, and the nature of the faculty.

The Freedom of Academia. For faculty and students in academic institutions, there is a form of freedom that is uncommon in other work organizations or social institutions. Most managers in business, officers in military units, administrators in government agencies, and officials in religious institutions are accountable in ways that are not applicable to academia. Academic freedom, though it may be challenged (Metzger, 1982), has real functional value in the generation and dissemination of knowledge as well as in debate on matters of knowledge and values. It does pose unique challenges for those administrators who must influence, and to some degree manage, support, and develop these faculty members. Academic freedom should not be confused with license to be irresponsible, as in the case of the tenured nonperformer (Henry, 1980). Two of the prices of academic freedom are the responsibilities to create new knowledge and to repay society's heavy investment in protecting independent thought (Freedman, 1986).

The Complexity of Academic Institutions. Although there is a diversity of institutional types in academia (for example, two-year versus four-year), individual universities and colleges are also quite internally complex. For example, some colleges are oriented more to pure and basic research, and others are oriented more to applied research. The first category might include basic sciences and liberal arts, and the second category might encompass business and engineering. This affects the nature of demands to which faculty in these diverse colleges are subject as well as the available resources for coping with these demands.

Following this example, uncertainty in the research process and procurement of essential resources might be problematic for the pure disciplines. Developing and maintaining relationships with external constituencies with nonacademic objectives might be much more stressful for the applied disciplines (Miles, 1980). This complexity and diversity in academic institutions requires that preventive actions be tailored for a particular academic unit.

The Nature of the Faculty. Faculty members in academic institutions are no more homogeneous than the institutions themselves. Champion and Champion (1973) have found several differences between large university and small college faculties. Among the more important of the differences are those concerning orientation to research and teaching, with university faculty members more research-oriented and college faculty members more teaching-oriented. As Gmelch points out in Chapter Three, academic rank, gender, and tenure status influence the nature of stress to which faculty members are subject.

In considering faculty characteristics, there are four issues of concern: professionalism, social status, institutional investment, and gender. First, faculty members are professionals and thus have internalized norms of behavior and ethics that guide their actions (Wilensky, 1964). These norms vary somewhat by discipline, but in all cases they make faculty members resistant to local institutional actions that are at variance with specific professional norms. Second, the social status of faculty members tends to isolate them culturally because those with whom they are intellectually compatible tend not to be those with whom they are economically compatible.

Third, as Gappa points out in Chapter Four, part-time faculty members have needs different from those of full-time faculty members. The differences between these faculty groups are important in tailoring a preventive stress-management program. Finally, the differences between male and female faculty members are equally important from a prevention standpoint. For example, while the proportion of full-time female medical school faculty members is increasing, the distribution is uneven (Higgins, 1982). Furthermore, female faculty members are subject to unique professional stresses such as stereotyping and social isolation (Nelson and Quick, 1985).

Institutional Preventive Actions

Quick and Quick (1984a) discuss in some detail the strategies and methods that institutions may use for encouraging health and preventing unhealthy consequences of stress. Within the contexts of academia and design considerations, there are four preventive actions most appropriate to this discussion: participative management, flexible work schedules, career development, and social support.

Participative Management. Since its origins in the research of Lippitt (Lewin and others, 1939), much has been written about participative (or democratic) management. Because of the many associations with this label, it is crucial to define the term at the outset. The participative academic environment is *not* one in which everyone has equal status. In any institutional setting, some will have more formal or informal influence than others. It is also *not* an environment in which subordinates tell superiors what to do. Rather, it is an environment in which individuals participate in decision making and control activities within defined limits. The limits are set by administrators in negotiation with faculty and staff. Thus, the limits as to what constitutes participation will vary by institution as well as within each institution.

Academic institutions, as other professional forms of organization, are already organized for faculty participation through formal mechanisms such as assemblies, committees, and the faculty senate. As long as these structural mechanisms are not bypassed, faculty members will have the means to express themselves and exert influence.

Four studies support the effectiveness of participation as a preventive stress management approach (Hall and Savery, 1986; Karasek 1979; Lewin and others, 1939; Quick and Quick, 1984b). The mechanism for its effectiveness appears to be the control that participation gives a person in any work environment.

The uniqueness of each academic institution discourages statement of general rules for establishing a participative environment. The professionalism of the faculty is only one of many considerations; another is the administration's consideration of the proportion of faculty members with terminal degrees. Therefore, the process of implementing participative management is both an art and a science. It is an art because it requires the administrator to have feedback from the faculty, and a science because it is based on established research findings.

There are a number of questions that should be addressed in the process of establishing a participative academic environment. The answers should guide an administrator in determining parameters of participation.

1. What is the faculty's level of professional development?

2. What are the decision areas of major concern to the faculty?
3. What decisions will have the most impact on the faculty?
4. How much participation does the faculty want?
5. What is the current level of achievement motivation within the faculty?
6. What decision areas should the faculty *not* participate in? Why?

As a general rule, participative management leads to the establishment of a healthier academic environment with lower levels of unresolved distress because faculty members are given increased control in a participative environment. The issue of control is often central for anyone who must manage stress. Control is achieved not only through participative management but also through flexible work schedules.

Flexible Work Schedules. Work in the United States has often been defined in terms of time because of the emphasis on labor-intensive work. The advent of information- and service-oriented work has changed this definition. Flexible work schedules have become increasingly common (Ronen, 1981). Because of the freedom of academic life and faculty professionalism, it would be dysfunctional to use time as a feature of job design. That does not alleviate the academician from accountability; it simply places the accountability in contexts other than time.

Although there is a need for flexibility in the management of academic institutions, this flexibility extends to work schedules and hours. If the institution does not define academic faculty work in terms of weekly hours, then how should it define work? The appropriate alternative in an academic institution is to define work in terms of specific outcomes and results without regard to time. Faculty members in particular would then be accountable for achieving certain specific, actual results agreed on between faculty members and administrators. This is essentially the results-oriented approach used by Drucker (1954) and often used today in many academic institutions. Results-orientation creates stress, and the flexible work schedule gives faculty members the control necessary to effectively manage the resulting achievement stress. Freedman (1986) discusses the professor's obligations in implementing this approach.

If academic work is defined in terms of results, then in what areas should results be established? Results should be specified in three broad categories: research, teaching, and service. The proportional commitment to each area by specific institutions, academic units, and individuals must be addressed. The institution must decide on its dominant focus and allow academic units and individual faculty members to adapt themselves accordingly. For example, one institution might commit itself to a distribution of 40 percent research, 40 percent teaching, and 20 percent service, and another may prefer 50 percent teaching, 25 percent service, and 25 percent research.

Within the institutionally established standards, some variety is required. A stimulating and healthy environment must be maintained. This means that there must be a mixture of talents within academic units that allows some people greater teaching emphasis and others greater research emphasis. The tolerance of such diversity, along with the need to make faculty and staff accountable for results, not time schedules, does complicate the administrator's task in several ways. However, the long-term benefits outweigh the short-term costs, and this approach is consistent with the fifth principle of preventive stress management, which concerns the dynamic nature of organizational life.

Career Development. Although it is true that organizations are dynamic and ever-changing, so, too, are people. An academic career poses opportunities and stresses and dilemmas. An academic institution is a dual organization, in some ways similar to a hospital, having administrative and professional components, which complicates the provision of opportunities for individual career development. The institution should therefore provide opportunities for administrators and professional colleagues (see Chapter One).

During the first decade of an academician's career, there are several key decisions that have long-term implications: promotion, tenure, and graduate faculty status. These will vary in significance by institution, and other decisions may be important at specific institutions. The most stress-relevant aspects of these decision processes are their predictability and consistency over time. Senior colleagues should be specific about their expectations for positive outcomes at various decision points. In addition, they should provide criticism concerning a junior colleague's progress at least once a year. However, career mastery at one point does not ensure it at a later point in the career (Hall, 1976).

Failure to cultivate the careers of young academicians will be costly for an institution in terms of good human resources and later payoffs. The culmination of an academician's career can also be a problem for an institution if it is not managed well. Discarding people prematurely should be avoided. Academic institutions are not the only organizations that employ a tenuring procedure, although they are among the most visible users. Henry (1980) has addressed the problem of unmotivated and unproductive medical school faculty who "retire" (on the job) after tenure is granted. He recommends modifying the tenuring procedure, withdrawing institutional support, and refusing merit salary increments. These recommendations would greatly encourage the successful young faculty member to continue a productive career. As Gmelch points out in Chapter Three, reward systems are a key stressor for the faculty. However, this stress need not necessarily be distress.

Managing the career development systems of an academic institution means monitoring opportunities and providing for a functional amount of turnover. New faculty members can be a vital asset to any department, stimulating those already there. In addition to adding new faculty members, the institution must commit resources to providing professional development opportunities for the faculty. New ideas, techniques, methods, and materials not only aid career development but they also bring into the institution new resources and energy that increases its health and vitality (Alderfer, 1976).

There are a number of key questions that faculty members and administrators must address concerning effective management of the institution's career development systems. For professional colleagues:

1. Are there clear, consistent standards for decisions concerning promotion, graduate faculty status, and tenure?
2. Historically, have decisions been made that are consistent with these standards?
3. Do junior faculty members receive clear, frequent criticism of their early career progress?
4. Are faculty members encouraging the advancement of each other's careers?

For administrators:

1. Are good procedures established for recruiting new faculty members?
2. Are career renewal opportunities available for established faculty members (see Chapter Nine)?
3. Are procedures established for remotivating or removing non-contributing faculty members?
4. Is the age, tenure, and expected attrition of the various institutional units monitored?

Good career development activities in an institution can serve to create necessary stress for faculty and staff and will provide channels and resources for the management of that stress.

Social Support. No one can successfully progress through life alone. Social support systems and those who are a part of them can contribute significantly to the management of the stress of academic life. House (1981) has shown that there are a variety of types of social support and that they may operate in different ways. I will discuss three types of social support: structural, informational, and appraisal support. Figure 1 supplies definitions and examples of each type of support.

The first form of social support is structural. A department chair can play a crucial role in affecting faculty stress by using a particular leadership style. Although the chair's role can be a key support for the faculty structurally, it is important to consider that the chair can be a help or a hindrance, depending on how he or she performs the role. When enacted effectively, the chair's role can be one of the most effective structural supports in the formal institution. A second key structural support for the faculty is the presence of necessary staff personnel—computer spe-

Figure 1. Social Support in Academic Institutions

Type	Faculty Illustration
Structural Support Providing a faculty member with formal mechanisms for performing the work role and coping with work demands.	Library staff members are able to procure various articles, books, and citations needed for a research project.
Information Support Providing a faculty member with information that can be used to cope with work demands.	A faculty member obtains criteria for promotion and tenure.
Appraisal Support Providing a faculty member with evaluative information regarding effectiveness in coping with work demands.	A faculty member obtains results of a review process for his or her promotion.

cialists, librarians, graduate assistants and others—who are able to perform specific tasks more efficiently than the individual faculty member. These structural supports enable the faculty member to meet job demands more effectively.

The second form of social support is information. Without accurate, timely information institutions cannot function effectively. It is the institution's responsibility to establish information channels for the distribution of crucial information, such as health plans, procedural matters concerning students, achievements of colleagues across the institution, grant opportunities, and key public matters. Key questions pertaining here are: (1) What do faculty members need to know? (2) how quickly do they need to know it? and (3) what is the most effective way to tell them?

The third form of social support is appraisal. Faculty members need criticism of their performance. Feedback should originate from four sources: administrators, colleagues, students, and selected professionals outside the institution. This appraisal is especially important in career development activities because it allows the faculty or staff member to alter unproductive behavior.

Appraisal support is also important for faculty members in that they can determine equity and consistency of reward allocation decisions. As Henry (1980) points out, reward allocation should be based on merit. It is also important that appraisal support activities be linked to work outcomes. Faculty and staff members need to know that evaluations have been conducted in their best interests as well as those of the institution.

Conclusion

Stress is an inevitable characteristic of academic life, but it need not become distress. Institutional preventive stress management is an organizational philosophy aimed at encouraging individual and institutional health while averting individual and institutional distress. To implement institutional preventive stress management requires an understanding of the peculiarities and the uniqueness of the institution and those who work within it. It is the freedom and diversity of academic institutions as well as the characteristics of its faculty that make it unique. Administrators can consider this uniqueness and still take preventive action to ensure the health and vitality of the institution and those within it. These preventive actions include implementing participative management, flexible work schedules, career development activities, and social support systems.

References

Alderfer, C. P. "Change Processes in Organizations." In M. D. Dunnette (ed.), *Handbook of Industrial and Organizational Psychology*. Skokie, Ill.: Rand McNally, 1976.

Champion, L. J., and Champion, D. J. "A Comparative Study of Large University and Small College Faculty." *Southern Journal of Educational Research*, 1973, 7 (3), 114-126.

Drucker, P. F. "Management by Objectives and Self-Control." In P. F. Drucker, *The Practice of Management*. New York: Harper & Row, 1954.

Freedman, J. O. "Point of View: The Professor's Life, Though Rarely Clear to Outsiders Has Its Rewards—and Its Costs." *Chronicle of Higher Education*, February 19, 1986, p. 92.

Hall, D. T. *Careers in Organizations*. Santa Monica, Calif.: Goodyear, 1976.

Hall, K., and Savery, L. K. "Tight Rein, More Stress." *Harvard Business Review*, 1986, 64 (1), 160-164.

Henry, J. B. "The Tenured Professor Syndrome." *Journal of Medical Education*, 1980, 55 (5), 449-451.

Higgins, E. "Women Faculty Members at U.S. Medical Schools." *Journal of Medical Education*, 1982, 57 (3), 202-203.

House, J. S. *Work Stress and Social Support*. Reading, Mass.: Addison-Wesley, 1981.

Karasek, R. A. "Job Demands, Job Decision Latitude, and Mental Strain: Implications for Job Redesign." *Administrative Science Quarterly*, 1979, 24, 285-308.

Lewin, K., Lippitt, R., and White, R. K. "Patterns of Aggressive Behavior in Experimentally Created 'Social Climates.' " *Journal of Social Psychology*, 1939, 10, 271-299.

Metzger, W. *Professors in Trouble: The Struggle for Academic Freedom in 20th-Century America*. Washington, D.C.: American Association of University Professors, 1982.

Miles, R. H. "Organizational Boundary Roles." In C. L. Cooper and R. Payne (eds.), *Current Concerns in Organizational Stress*. New York: Wiley, 1980.

Nelson, D. L., and Quick, J. C. "Professional Women: Are Distress and Disease Inevitable?" *Academy of Management Review*, 1985, 10 (2), 206-218.

84

Quick, J. C., and Quick, J. D. *Organizational Stress and Preventive Management.* New York: McGraw-Hill, 1984a.

Quick, J. C., and Quick, J. D. "Preventive Stress Management at the Organizational Level." *Personnel,* 1984b, *61* (5), 24-34.

Ronen, S. *Flexible Working Hours: An Innovation in the Quality of Work.* New York: McGraw-Hill, 1981.

Wilensky, H. L. "The Professionalization of Everyone?" *American Journal of Sociology,* 1964, *52* (2), 137-158.

James C. Quick is associate professor of organizational behavior at the University of Texas at Arlington, and former president of the Arlington Unit Board, American Heart Association.

*A creative renewal program, designed by and for the faculty
at the University of Georgia, has proven to be a promising
approach to instructional improvement and faculty
development.*

The Faculty Renewal Program
at the University of Georgia

Ronald D. Simpson, William K. Jackson

In 1985 the University of Georgia (UGA) became the first public institution of higher education in the United States to engage in a bicentennial
celebration. By securing a charter in 1785, Georgia became the first state to
allocate resources for a publicly supported institution of higher learning.
By the mid 1960s UGA had grown into a large regional university with
equivalent missions of teaching, research, and service.

In 1967 the Georgia state legislature increased the budget of UGA
by almost 100 percent. The number of faculty members rose from 1,200 to
1,800, and the new chancellor of the University System of Georgia and
UGA's new president clearly indicated that they intended to transform
UGA into a major research university. During the ensuing decade the
nature of the institution changed dramatically. The administration effected
a stringent promotion system and publicized the expectation that faculty
members be productive in research. By the mid 1970s UGA was recognized
as one of the major research universities in the country (Carnegie Council
on Policy Studies in Higher Education, 1978).

In an effort to increase emphasis on instruction, the vice-president
for academic affairs decided in 1979 to create the Office of Instructional
Development. In 1981 the first permanent director was hired following a
nationwide search. Since that time a wide range of instructional and fac-

P. Seldin (ed.). *Coping with Faculty Stress.*
New Directions for Teaching and Learning, no. 29. San Francisco: Jossey-Bass, Spring 1987.

ulty development activities has been tried (Jackson and Simpson, 1984). In facing the challenge of improving instruction at a major research university, the director and associate director have attempted to create programs that address both the professional and the personal needs of the faculty (Simpson and Jackson, 1984). The following description is an account of what we believe is one of the most promising approaches to instructional and faculty development that has been witnessed in higher education.

Assessing Needs

In establishing the Office of Instructional Development (OID) the vice-president for academic affairs (VPAA), the senior vice-president at UGA, made two critical decisions. First, the office would report directly to the VPAA. Second, the OID would be advised by a carefully selected faculty committee representing the university's thirteen schools and colleges. During the first two years, when most of the current programs were initiated, the director and associate director relied heavily on faculty input. In fact, the Instructional Advisory Committee (IAC) has become perhaps the most prestigious and active committee on campus.

Much of the actual work by the IAC is accomplished through sub-committees. One of the subcommittees attends to faculty development matters, and like other subcommittees, this group is free to consult additional resource persons. Two resource persons, a professor of philosophy and a professor of counseling psychology, proved to be key providers of input. At a meeting composed of these two faculty members and the director and associate director, they decided to initiate activities that would improve the quality of life at UGA by preventing the burnout that often accompanies the creative endeavors of teaching and research. A subsequent meeting led to the establishment of special planning committee to further investigate these ideas.

A superlative planning committee was established. The group was composed not only of strong faculty members, including the two mentioned previously, but also key administrators in the helping professions. For example, directors from the Psychology Clinic, Counseling and Testing Center, and Fitness Center were members, as were faculty members from such disciplines as recreation and leisure studies, health education, and psychology. The fourteen-member committee met every three to four weeks beginning in November 1982. Full attendance was common and an unusual rapport within the group quickly emerged.

The committee spent several hours establishing a philosophy and guidelines for its work. One cornerstone was that these efforts would be "by the faculty, for the faculty" and that developing a concept of community would be a primary goal. In assessing several development strategies, the committee decided to sponsor a conference in September just before the opening of school. In spring 1983 the committee distributed a list of thirty suggested topics to the 4,200 faculty and professional staff members. Responses from the survey were analyzed and the committee, using this and other indirect measures, organized a conference based on faculty needs. The vice-president for academic affairs endorsed the conference, which was supported with both staff and financial assistance by the Office of Instructional Development.

The First Conference

Although deliberations of this committee initially grew out of a concern about professional burnout, stress in academia, and other phenomena relating to current challenges in higher education, the group agreed from the outset that their efforts should be positive in nature. Hence, the concept of renewal was adapted. It was also felt, particularly after surveying the faculty, that both professional and personal aspects of renewal should be addressed. With this general concept in mind, the committee added other important attributes that they hoped the conference could embody. Some of these major themes included the following:

1. Topics in the conference should address the needs of young, mid-career, and preretirement faculty members.

2. The tone of the sessions should be positive and action-oriented, with such topics as "coping with performance pressures," "improving interpersonal communication," and "managing your personal finances."

3. Because spouses are an important part of the university community, they should be invited to the conference.

4. The conference itself should be viewed only as a starting point; therefore, follow-up sessions throughout the year should be available for interested faculty and spouses.

5. Presenters should be for the most part from the UGA faculty; the concept of "faculty helping faculty" should become a recurring theme.

6. Conference attendees should be asked to preregister and should have an opportunity to select a first and second choice for each concurrent session.

7. All presenters should donate their services to the university, and all attendees should pay a small fee to cover food and other conference costs.

With these themes serving as guideposts, the committee planned a one-day conference that was held after Labor Day and before the beginning of classes in fall 1983. Each participant paid $15 to attend the event. During the late afternoon of the first day over forty faculty, staff, and spouses displayed their leisure time interests and activities in a hobby fair. This fair proved to be a successful event and was well attended. A banquet was held after the hobby fair and Bill Foster, head basketball coach at the University of South Carolina, delivered an appropriate address in which he shared with the audience life changes he had made as a result of a recent and nationally publicized heart attack.

Over 250 people participated in the first conference. Over half completed evaluation forms, which were reviewed by a conference evaluation specialist, who reported his findings to the committee. Response to the conference was overwhelmingly positive. The highlights were the outstanding variety of topics, the high quality of session instruction, follow-up opportunities accompanying each session, the banquet address, and the hobby fair. Most of those who attended agreed that the conference was refreshing, worthwhile, and an activity that the university should continue.

Follow-up activities during the remainder of the 1983–84 academic year included advanced workshops, special training courses, discussion groups, articles in campus publications, and regularly scheduled seminars. The planning committee also voted unanimously to begin planning a second conference.

Renewal Conferences II and III

With only minor changes in planning committee membership, the group began planning a second conference in early fall 1983. One new committee member suggested that the new conference be called Renewal II, subtitled Second Conference on Professional and Personal Renewal. This suggestion was adopted, and the titles of Renewal II and Renewal III were used thereafter. In addition, the planning committee agreed that Renewal II should be built on the strength of the first conference (hereafter referred to as Renewal I), with only minor changes made. In a second survey of the faculty, thirty-seven topics were listed for faculty members and spouses to check the six sessions they would most like to attend if they participated in Renewal II.

Relatively few changes were made. The keynote address was delivered by university President Fred C. Davison, who used this opportunity to focus on faculty development issues. A faculty member then discussed results from a health-risk appraisal form that had been distributed to those who had preregistered. The analysis of this survey in which each person assessed his or her health was one of the most popular sessions of the conference. In an effort to attract more spouses, a third round of concurrent sessions was scheduled the evening of the first day. A closing luncheon replaced Renewal I's evening banquet. Well-known columnist, author, and university alumnus Lewis Grizzard spoke after a brief presentation by the vice-president for academic affairs.

Evaluation procedures for Renewal II were similar to those used in Renewal I and evaluations from Renewal II were even more positive. Attendance was 10 percent higher with the nonduplicated count for the two conferences being approximately 350. The concurrent sessions received high ratings, and improvements such as the president's keynote address, additional sessions scheduled in the evening, shifting the banquet to a second-day luncheon, concluding with an upbeat and humorous speaker, and refining concurrent sessions using feedback from Renewal I contributed to Renewal II's success.

The planning committee met after Renewal II to decide whether or not these efforts, including follow-up opportunities, should continue. Plans for Renewal III were then begun. The planning committee membership increased from fifteen to nineteen, and six original committee members remained. The basic philosophy remained intact and relatively few changes were made. Renewal III's topics are listed in Figure 1. The figure indicates topics repeated from previous conferences and first-time topics. Based on the success of the two previous hobby fairs, a health fair and a university fair were added. The health fair included displays and demonstrations by university health educators on topics relating to diet, exercise, mental health, and other dimensions of general health and safety. The university fair included displays from over fifty units on campus that offer goods and services to faculty and family members. A booklet containing over 150 university services was compiled and distributed to all Renewal III participants.

In addition, the second day was extended to a full program, which provided time for another round of longer and more in-depth concurrent sessions. For example, a panel on human relations was able to examine racial issues on campus unrestricted by a seventy-five-minute time frame. A three-hour seminar for department heads also benefited from the expansion.

Evaluation responses for Renewal III indicated even greater success. Three factors contributed. First, refining selection of concurrent session topics and presenters led to even higher ratings. Using preregistration information to make last-minute changes also helped eliminate sessions that might be poorly attended. Second, the great variety of opportunities available at the joint exhibitions of the hobby, health, and university fairs contributed to Renewal III's success. Third, Renewal III was held in a facility with a commons area capable of accommodating large numbers of displays and activities.

Two features did not improve. One of the major speakers received lower ratings, and attendance dropped by about 10 percent. Because most of those attracted to this type of event had presumably already attended, and because the three conferences were strikingly similar, it was not surprising that a drop in attendance would ultimately occur. In a postconference planning committee evaluation meeting, written and verbal evaluation indicated that the quality of each renewal conference had improved and that the participants felt that they had taken part in an unusual experience.

The National Conference on Professional and Personal Renewal

Figure 1. The 1985 University of Georgia
Renewal Conference Session Topics

Burnout[a]	Panel on Human Relations: Bridging the Gap
Change in Marriage and Family Life	Physical Fitness[a]
Creating Interest Groups	Positively Single
Creative Collaboration	Professional, Personal, and Community Responsibilities
Decision Making and Problem Solving	Publishers' Contracts and Scholars' Rights
Developing a Quality of Life	Recreation and Renewal
Effective Tax-Planning Strategies	Relaxation[a]
Enhancing Control of Life-style and Work-style	Retirement as Renewal
Enhancing Self-Esteem[a]	Seminar for Department Heads
Financial Planning[a]	Stress Management[a]
Interpersonal Communication[a]	Stress Management at Home
Learning Styles and Expectations of Adults	Tax-Sheltered Annuities, Insurance for Retirement
Managing Interpersonal Conflicts	The Excitement of Teaching
Microcomputers[a]	The One-Minute Manager[a]
Nontraditional Students	Three Views of the Future
Organizations and Stress	Time Management[a]

[a]These topics were repeated from one or both of the previous conferences.

for faculty has evolved from these conferences. Supported in part by the Teachers Insurance Annuity Association and the American Association for Higher Education, the University of Georgia hosted this conference, which was held in Atlanta on April 10–12, 1986. The conference brought together over fifty presenters from across the country to share ideas and experiences designed to provide renewal opportunities for faculty members in colleges and universities. The keynote speaker at this conference was John W. Gardner, former secretary of the U.S. Department of Health, Education, and Welfare and author of *Self-Renewal*.

From a meeting of a few concerned faculty members in 1982, three successful on-campus renewal conferences and one national conference have emerged. From the collective ideas of several sensitive and creative persons has come a movement that is likely to spread to other campuses and organizations. In terms of the broad array of activities in instructional and faculty development that we have tried, the concept of promoting personal, professional, and institutional renewal seems to rank as perhaps the most fundamental and effective of all approaches.

Reflections and Recommendations

During the past five years the University of Georgia has experimented with over two dozen programs and activities designed to enhance effective teaching and promote faculty development. Some have been more successful than others. Probably no single program has changed the character of this institution as much as the three renewal conferences held on campus. It has not only been the most satisfying endeavor in which we have engaged, it has contributed the most to developing a sense of community—a community that values teaching and values the worth of its individuals. Because this is one of the premier goals of instructional and faculty development at UGA, it is not difficult to understand why this particular program has received such high marks.

In reflecting on the many positive notes, one of the most important characteristics of this endeavor had been that of allowing the rich thinking of the faculty to come to the forefront. One senior faculty member on the planning committee remarked that in twenty-five years of committee work, this one had been by far the best. The committee operated in an open, democratic, and creative manner, and those who served on it felt that their hard work had led to something of value that was appreciated.

In making recommendations to those on other campuses, one important item is to include the expertise and credibility of the faculty in developing and implementing such a program. Another attribute of the planning committee was its creative nature. This group promoted risk-taking, which in turn led to a full spectrum of ideas once any topic came up for discussion.

Another cornerstone of the conferences that we felt was significant was the inclusion of spouses. So often organizations fail to recognize the importance of the family to the total well-being of the individual (see Chapter Five). By allowing faculty and staff to attend to the personal as well as the professional sides of their lives, a more honest experience can emerge.

Another important aspect of this program was the follow-up activities. As one committee member said at the outset, "Renewal cannot be properly facilitated with a mere one-day conference. It must be ongoing." The various seminars and workshops that have allowed the renewal conference attendees to go into more depth with certain topics have been invaluable. The follow-up activities have been varied in format, offered at different times, and well publicized. Therefore, any faculty member or spouse with special needs or interests can find throughout the year extended opportunities for learning, sharing, and growing. We recommend that this be an integral part of any faculty renewal program.

One necessary component of any faculty development program is that of obtaining support from the senior administration, which means involving administrators in the planning, implementation, and evaluation phases. More important, this means allowing presidents and vice-presidents to share in the successes. All too often the successes are focused on people and the failures on administration. When the central administration makes sizable allocations for programs, they are in fact building the potential for something good to happen. When programs do well, it is only logical that the administration's contributions should be acknowledged. At UGA the president and senior vice-president have been involved with the three renewal conferences as well as with the national conference. It has been an excellent opportunity to thank them for their support and, more important, to allow them to join in and enjoy a valuable and pleasant experience. We believe that this is a key to success.

It is difficult to predict where the renewal conference concept will take us at UGA. Plans are being made for a second national conference, this time for faculty members who may wish to come for their own professional and personal growth. The planning committee is continuing to examine other options for the campus. Are there other times of the year we should try? Would restricting the conference to one day allow more people to attend? Should there be more specific themes attached to future conferences? Are there other formats that should be tried? These and other questions are now being asked and discussed. One concern that we have not adequately addressed is how to attract those on the faculty who are reluctant to participate in activities outside their own speciality area or department. We have noted that attendance has been somewhat uneven across the disciplines and professions. Faculty and staff from the helping professions and service areas have attended more regularly than those from the humanities and natural sciences. We suspect, moreover, that some who need this experience the most may be the most reluctant to come. We have not found a formula for solving this problem.

What does seem clear to us is that a college or university represents a rich collection of talent. When properly mobilized, this knowledge and assortment of skills can be shared across departmental lines and disciplines. This is when an institution becomes more than a place of work. This is when it becomes a community. This is when people not only give but also receive. This refueling of mind and spirit is what renewal is all about.

References

Carnegie Council on Policy Studies in Higher Education. *Classification of Institutions of Higher Education.* Berkeley, Calif.: Carnegie Council on Policy Studies in Higher Education, 1978.

Jackson, W. K., and Simpson, R. D. "The Office of Instructional Development as a Center for Personal, Professional, and Organizational Renewal." *Journal of Staff, Program, and Organization Development,* 1984, *2* (1), 12–15.

Simpson, R. D., and Jackson, W. K. "Promoting Professional and Personal Renewal." *Improving College and University Teaching*, 1984, *32* (4), 200-202.

Ronald D. Simpson is professor of science education and director of the Office of Instructional Development at the University of Georgia. His research on how student feelings relate to the learning of science has influenced his approach to improving instruction at a comprehensive research university.

William K. Jackson is associate director of the Office of Instructional Development at the University of Georgia. He was assistant academic dean at Presbyterian College, Clinton, South Carolina, a liberal arts college known for its excellence in instruction, and he has been involved in planning faculty development activities for more than ten years.

Index

A

Abel, E. K., 36, 37, 38, 39, 41
Academia: complexity of, 77; faculty in, 77–78; freedom of, 76; nature of, 76–78; supermen and superwomen in, 46
Academics. *See* Faculty
Adams, J. D., 14, 15, 16, 20, 53, 62
Adams, R. D., 20
Administrators: evaluation of faculty performance by, 17; interaction of, with faculty, 18, 30; responsibility of, for stress management, 75–82
Alderfer, C. P., 81, 83
Alexander, L., 17, 20
American Association for Higher Education (AAHE), 15, 90
American Association of University Professors (AAUP), 16
Anderson, R. E., 14, 20
Armour, R. A., 1, 3, 11

B

Baldwin, R. G., 15, 20
Bender, R. C., 16, 20
Benjamin, E., 16
Benson, H., 69, 72
Bess, J., 15, 20
Biglan, A., 24, 26, 31
Blackburn, R. T., 15, 20, 27, 29, 31
Blackwell, M. W., 16, 20
Bowen, H. R., 11, 15, 20
Bower, G. A., 59, 62
Bower, S. A., 59, 62
Boyer, E., 16, 18, 20
Brief, A. P., 37, 41
Brown, B. B., 53, 56, 62
Burnout: as academic malaise, 4–5; definition of, 5; institutional response to faculty, 7–10; nonclinical, 10. *See also* Stress

C

Caffarella, R. S., 1, 3, 11
California Community College system, 38

California State Postsecondary Education Commission, 36, 38, 42
California State University system, 38
Career: balancing, with life demands, 47–48; and children, 47–48; control over, 10; development, 80–81; early retirement from, 8–9; family obligations and, 15, 43–52; goals of faculty, 6–7, 17, 28–30; planning programs, 8; seamlessness of, 45; shifts, 8; success of faculty, 6–7
Cares, R. C., 29, 31
Carnegie Council on Policy Studies in Higher Education, 85, 92
Carnegie Foundation for the Advancement of Teaching, 4, 10, 14, 16, 18
Carter, K. R., 60, 63
Catalyst, 50, 52
Champion, D. J., 77, 83
Champion, L. J., 77, 83
Chronicle of Higher Education, The, 16, 20
Clagett, C., 15, 20
Clark, B. R., 4, 11
College of Charleston, career development program at, 7
Consortium Professorships, 8
Cooperative Program for the Professional Renewal of Faculty (COPROF), 8

D

de Guzman, R. M., 5, 11, 13, 16, 18, 20, 34, 35, 42
Dembo, T., 31
DESC script, 59
Drucker, P. F., 79, 83

E

Eble, K. E., 4, 11
Ellis, A., 61, 63

F

Faculty Resource Network, 8
Faculty Stress Index (FSI), 26